PRAISE FOR *INFLUENCING*

"This book is for everyone who wants to understand the psyche of how people are making buying decisions in a rapidly changing world. Rebecca and Devora give you an MBA in a book. It will accelerate your understanding of what works today in influencing shopper decisions, and it will surprise you!"
Nadia Bilchik, CNN Editorial Producer and global speaker

"Today, consumers have more choices than ever before. If your company wants to keep up—and thrive—in a world transformed by the near-infinite number of online options, read this book."
Dorie Clark, author of *The Long Game* and Executive Education Faculty, Duke University's Fuqua School of Business

"In *Influencing Shopper Decisions*, Rebecca and Devora have managed to produce a book that is compelling, evidence-based and tells a great story. It's packed with examples, first-hand experiences and fresh thinking about how the internet has so radically changed our shopping attitudes and behavior and all our mindsets, both as consumers and branding professionals. Their narrative includes a large dose of the real world, and why it is so important to recognize the limitations that blinkered 'brand narcissism' causes for brand owners. Real people don't care about your marketing plans. They only care about how you can help their lives. This book makes a great contribution to the sum of brand knowledge."
Rita Clifton CBE, global brand expert, Former Chair of Interbrand and Portfolio Chair, Board Director and Former Vice Chair at Saatchi & Saatchi

"Building on the latest research in agile neuroscience, *Influencing Shopper Decisions* clearly explains how consumers make choices about what products and services to purchase and how you can use these insights to build a stronger brand and win more customers."
Jeff DeGraff, Professor and coauthor of *The Innovation Code* and *The Creative Mindset*

"What the industrial revolution did for agriculture, online shopping has done for retail. And it happened so fast. Choices exploded and we could get lost in a sea of products and services. Thankfully, *Influencing Shopper Decisions* provides insight from two of the foremost experts in the field. The past, the present, and the future are laid out beautifully. You will love this book!"
Chester Elton, bestselling coauthor of *The Carrot Principle*, *Leading with Gratitude*, and *Anxiety at Work*

"If you sell something (and who doesn't?), Rebecca and Devora have studied your category and can help you make sense of the current mindsets of shoppers. From strategies to tactics, these pages are chock-full of actionable ways to reach, serve, and delight consumers in our ever-changing world."
Kristi Faulkner, President, WOMENK!ND

"Whether you're a CPG brand marketer, digital media company, or small business owner, this book will help you understand the new shopper. I appreciated that it was easy to understand and provided actions businesses could take. Rebecca and Devora coach you through keeping your brand relevant."
Marshall Goldsmith, new member of the Thinkers50 Hall of Fame and the only two-time Thinkers50 #1 Leadership Thinker in the World

"If you are serious about customer experience, then read this book to get inside your customer's head and understand how they truly think about making a purchase. When you understand how a customer buys, you can develop a better CX strategy to elevate your business and brand."
Shane Green, CX Consultant and author of *Culture Hacker*

"First and foremost, you must know what your customers want and expect. This is the guide to understanding how your customers think, how they buy, and what influences them. Read this before your competition does!"
Shep Hyken, customer experience expert and author of *I'll Be Back: How to Get Customers to Come Back Again and Again*

"Online shopping has stripped away loyalty and brand fidelity. *Influencing Shopper Decisions* provides the most updated shopper journey insights today. It exposes all of us for the kind of shoppers we've become and how we've screwed with corporate marketing mentalities."
Charlene Li, *New York Times* bestselling author of *The Disruption Mindset* and founder of Altimeter

"In *Influencing Shopper Decisions*, Brooks and Rogers blow the roof off traditional, narcissistic brand standards and research methods. Now is the time to think like a Mindful Marketer and DIAL into your buyer's true beliefs and values. Want to be a modern, mindful marketer? Follow their lead."
Lisa Nirell, author, CMO whisperer, 100 Coaches member, and livestream host

"Researchers Rebecca Brooks and Devora Rogers bring an unparalleled understanding of the shopper mindset and the keys to unlocking it. No matter what kind of business professional you are, you must read this book to stay current with the market. Nobody explains the nature of the new shopper, and how to reach them, like these two experts do."
Peter Shankman, bestselling author of *Faster Than Normal: Unlocking the Gifts of the ADHD Brain and Zombie Loyalists: Using Great Service to Create Rabid Fans*

Influencing Shopper Decisions

Unleash the Power of Your Brand
to Win Customers

Rebecca Brooks
Devora Rogers

KoganPage

First published in Great Britain and the United States in 2022 by Kogan Page Limited

2nd Floor, 45 Gee Street	8 W 38th Street, Suite 902	4737/23 Ansari Road
London	New York, NY 10018	Daryaganj
EC1V 3RS	USA	New Delhi 110002
United Kingdom		India
www.koganpage.com		

© Rebecca Brooks and Devora Rogers 2022

ISBNs

Hardback   9781398603639
Paperback   9781398603615
Ebook   9781398603622

British Library Cataloguing-in-Publication Data

A CIP record for this book is available from the British Library.

Library of Congress Control Number

2022931294

Typeset by Hong Kong FIVE Workshop
Print production managed by Jellyfish
Printed and bound by CPI Group (UK) Ltd, Croydon CR0 4YY

Kogan Page books are printed on paper from sustainable forests.

CONTENTS

FOREWORD
Lisa Bodell
Bestselling author of *Kill the Company* and *Why Simple Wins*

If there was one word to describe the past couple of years, it would be "disruption." Our families were disrupted. Our careers were disrupted. Our very lives were disrupted. While that may seem to have a negative connotation, disruption is sometimes good—particularly when it causes positive change, new ways of thinking and innovation in our businesses.

As I often say, "Being stuck in the status quo causes us to lose our ability to think." Market research has been built on a foundation of practices from 100 years ago and only modified or tweaked since. But the advent of digital shopping means that shoppers are no longer thinking and behaving the way they used to.

Today, brands must understand and unlock the shopper brain in new ways. You might want to read that again. Think about your own buying patterns and you'll know it's true. When I first started reading this book, I thought, "The world has changed, yes, yes, yes." Then, as I became engrossed in the narrative, I realized just how much the world has changed. All of us shop... for everything, and we now do it differently.

However, market research tools haven't evolved, so they are giving brands incorrect information and insights. That doesn't work for Rebecca Brooks and Devora Rogers. This dynamic duo is fascinated by the way the digital world is transforming the way we approach marketing, branding, and research. Together they co-developed the methodology deployed for Google's groundbreaking ZMOT research, and they've provided truly amazing insights not only for sales and marketing professionals, but for all business leaders. Forget everything you've learned about marketing. *Influencing Shopper Decisions* tells you what you need to know now and, more importantly, why it matters.

I have a keynote where I ask, "Winning innovators embrace change—do you?" I point out, like Brooks and Rogers do, that in so many organizations we've forgotten how to think differently. The very structures put in place inside organizations to help them grow all too often hold them back. To do better, we must be curious and rebuild for today's economy. This is especially true for the market research industry.

Unconventional ways of shopping, much of them driven by tech and ecommerce, have been slowly growing for years. Groceries delivered to your door, telemedicine, designing and buying a car, all possible online. But the pandemic turbocharged our need to evolve, shifting our thinking about these alternative shopping approaches from novelty to necessity. The 10—30 percent of purchases that were being made online before Covid-19 increased by more than 300 percent in some categories. New behaviors formed, resulting in even greater "Shopper Promiscuity"—an accurate and descriptive term Brooks and Rogers have coined for this new type of shopper behavior. Has your company kept up? If your position has anything to do with driving revenue, you must understand how your buyers are changing.

Encourage your employees to think differently and critically. Don't fall into "Brand Narcissism," as Brooks and Rogers describe it: "the brand wants to know about itself, but the consumer doesn't care about the brand at all." Brand Narcissism is a barrier to smarter thinking about shoppers. Brands that think like their shoppers do are the ones who stand the best chance of being successful. Market research, understanding buyers, hasn't had the radical change needed in the industry because executives fear change and are not fostering environments where curiosity and challenges to the status quo are encouraged.

While reading *Influencing Shopper Decisions*, I also realized how much my shopping habits have changed over the past decade. Me and everyone else! Fortunately, this book outlines specific strategies for brands to understand and manage Shopper Promiscuity, and how to use tactics that meet shoppers where they are.

Today, shoppers and consumers have more choices than ever before, which means they make hundreds of decisions a month about where and how to buy. This access and opportunity means shoppers are becoming "promiscuous"—meaningfully more open to new brands, products, and shopping channels. In this enlightened book, Brooks and Rogers bring an unparalleled understanding of the shopper mindset and the keys to unlocking it.

Did your dad subscribe to *Consumer Reports*, and would he avoid major purchases until he could consult it? Or maybe you knew someone else like that at some point in your life. Now, how many people, including yourself, do you know who must look at product reviews online for everything from a refrigerator to the cold-packed, organic pickles they're storing inside it? A marketing phenomenon was happening pre-Covid that snowballed during Covid and really, every businessperson needs to understand it.

Is your brand having trouble maintaining relevance and growing engagement with consumers? Perhaps you need to *unleash the power of your brand*. Fortunately, Brooks and Rogers have done the research and provided actionable ways to reach and serve consumers in our new world. This is the most important book you can read this year if you're in sales, marketing, or research.

In fact, if you've been running the marketing shop for a while, I'd like you to think about some things. What does your budget look like? How different is it from ten years ago, five years ago? After reading *Influencing Shopper Decisions*, I found myself asking even tougher questions. Should we advertise on TV? Is print really dead? What's the opportunity with augmented reality? Should we hire an influencer to create a video on YouTube? Or promote our goods through targeted ads on Facebook and Instagram? What do we do about TikTok?

Thank goodness this book provides the key questions consumers have that must be answered when they're in the shopper journey. It also provides answers on how your brand can stay relevant.

"Shopper Promiscuity" demonstrates to us that shoppers are changing radically. And, with the acceleration caused by Covid and the looming impact of Web 3.0, they will continue to change in new and fascinating ways. Brooks and Rogers are sounding the warning call that if the research industry doesn't change fast, it may become irrelevant.

Improving leadership, managing performance, maintaining customer service… None of it matters if your brand falls out of the market. So read books on that some other time. Read *Influencing Shopper Decisions* right now! This book is going to disrupt the practice of market research like social media changed the meaning of "friend."

ACKNOWLEDGEMENTS

We are keenly aware that none of this book would have been possible without the amazing support of our team at Alter Agents. They have picked up the slack on the days we were writing, fact checked us, triple checked the data, and most importantly, continued doing incredible work for clients. In particular, a big shout out to Clayton Southerly, who was our partner and co-editor and got the brunt of our neuroticism throughout the book writing process, our lead analyst on the shopper influence work, Drishti Saxena, Research Directors Xavier Alvarez and Lauren DeWitt Thompson, Alter Agents Managing Director Eddie Francis, and our General Manager, Carmen Schalk.

Thank you to John Ross for being the original inspiration for this work and for being a committed and supportive mentor to us all these years. Thank you to the Immersion team for being incredible partners, and in particular, to Laura Beavin-Yates for your contributions to the book.

Rebecca Brooks
I have no words adequate enough to express how grateful I am for all my family has done. All the credit goes to my husband, Douglas Goldstein. He's been a rock. Taking on the extra slack, reading chapters late into the night, encouraging me to keep going, and spending many nights solo parenting as I scuttled off to hotels to write. Most importantly, thank you to Doug for always making me laugh, no matter how exhausted I was. Charlie and Calvin, thank you for letting me spend so many nights away and miss time with you. Thank you for cheering me on and pretending to be excited when I wanted to share a milestone I'd reached. You are both hilarious and awesome and loving and sweet. I'm so lucky to be your mama.

Devora Rogers
Thank you to my parents, Deena, Randy, Tio, Janet, Eric, and Laurie. Thank you to my friends—my North Stars, my co-regulators, my ride-or-dies—thank you for listening to me as I made this journey, and for when I complained, for telling me to go back and sit down to write some more.

Thank you to my husband, Ethan, for giving me the space and time and support necessary to write this book. Thank you for giving me excellent ideas and useful critiques. Thank you for the midday and evening meals—the Ram-Don, the Tortillas Español, the grilled ribeyes, the pork dumplings, and the insanely good chicken and fish sandos you made possible so I could write.

And above all, thank you Eden for being, for being you, for being a bright light in the sometimes dark and windy universe. You inspire me every day and I love you.

LIST OF FIGURES

LIST OF TABLES

01

Redefining the Shopper Journey for the First Time

When people ask how we met, Devora likes to say that she and Rebecca got together and had a baby. And that baby was called ZMOT. Or, her full given name: *Zero Moment of Truth*. It was a kind of happy accident, a lucky break—a kismet—that launched our approach to understanding the shopper journey. It also shifted how brands thought about marketing in a new world where influencing shoppers could happen at any time, any place, any way, any how. We'll talk later in this chapter about what exactly the Google ZMOT study accomplished, but first let's step back just for a few moments to a world that looks pretty different from the one we inhabit today.

To understand the context of *our journey* to developing a new understanding of the *shopper journey*, we have to remember a time before smartphones, before Amazon's dominance, and before everything about the way we shop changed—and would continue to change at a dizzying pace, *forever*.

So, let's step back a moment in time.

The Internet Changed Everything

The National Science Foundation lifted the ban on commercial enterprise on the internet in 1995, and by the late 1990s the dot com boom was underway. It seemed every category had a tailored ".com" where you could buy the latest things—places like Pets.com, Webvan.com and eToys.com. Some legacy brands had ventured into ecommerce, but most brand websites were still glorified brochures. The few online shoppers that existed at the time shopped from their desktops, not mobile phones. Investor excitement over the novel nature of internet companies combined with monetary policy changes created a bubble where investors ignored traditional metrics of sound business in order to "get in on the ground floor." So a bunch of companies launched IPOs and raised a lot of cash without ever making an actual profit or, in some cases, any significant revenue. After a series of high-profile merger failures and increased interest rates, investors gained some clarity and the first dot com bubble burst. Less than 50 percent of dot com companies survived to 2004 (Berlin, 2008).

When those early brands went under in the dot com bust, marketers and advertisers breathed a sigh of relief. Their failure was evidence—*clear proof!*—that ecommerce was always going to be niche or, better yet, a passing anomaly. Traditional broadcast media and brick-and-mortar stores were unchanged, so they got back to business as usual. But the bust didn't take all of the ecommerce class down with it. By the end of the decade, the sector was emerging into what we could call its teenage form—more mature and a bit smarter, but still experiencing growing pains. Amazon and eBay had started taking on an increasing share of purchases and more brands were adding ecommerce options to their websites.

Still, the prevailing opinion of the time among retailers, brand managers, and marketers was that online was always going to be a small piece of the story. Maybe it would grow slowly to account for 10 percent or so of sales, but never anything more meaningful than that. And the people who shopped online were themselves niche. Any prudent marketer would stay focused on traditional channels for advertising and retail. However, a small group of marketers and researchers could see the vision and potential of ecommerce when it matured into a full-grown adult. And that "adulthood" was coming faster than most people realized.

Where We Started

That's where our story picks up, in the latter part of the "aughts", from about 2008 to 2010. Remember, we were still sending texts and emails from Blackberry devices—the iPhone had only just entered the marketplace. 4G was emerging but not widespread. Facebook had only 100 million users, not 2.6 billion (Associated Press, 2013). The latter figure is a third of all humans on the planet today, for those keeping track. Amazon was making $19 million in annual revenue, not $125 billion (MacroTrends, 2021).

In 2008, in the iconic art deco Fine Arts Building in downtown Los Angeles, Rebecca was hosting a group of consumer packaged goods (CPGs) brand executives who were struggling with her presentation. She was trying to convince them that her market research data on digital information sources was accurate. That, yes, people really did turn to online sources for information before they bought their ice cream.

Rebecca was paid by companies and ad agencies to reveal the voice of their customer through market research. *What did they love? What did they find frustrating? What products were they considering and why? How do we get them to buy our stuff again?* It was her job to make sure that the decision makers at her clients' companies knew exactly what the customer was experiencing.

Rebecca's academic background is in primatology, or the scientific study of non-human primates, and she had found a way to shift to studying human subjects by building a career in market research. Right before meeting Devora, she had left a job managing a $20 million branch for a large market research company to start her own firm. There were a lot of reasons behind that move, but prominent among them was that Rebecca was frustrated by the constraints imposed by traditional research methodologies. These methods had been developed decades before by people focused on the art of selling, but her interest was in the "whys" of the behavior. She was itching to try something new at her own company. Rebecca didn't know it at the time, but that move would give her the freedom and opportunity to connect with Devora a few months into her new role as a CEO and entrepreneur.

But back to that meeting Rebecca was sloughing through with ice cream executives. The other people around the table had a very clear opinion of who their customer was. The data that Rebecca had collected showed that 47 percent of shoppers were using a digital source before making a purchase. But the CPG executives didn't believe it. And they were not about to change their minds about who they *thought* their consumer was and what they *thought* these consumers were doing before purchase. With the meeting about to really fall apart, Rebecca switched tactics and asked people at the table to talk about their most recent purchase, whatever they felt comfortable sharing. She heard stories about razors, a new armchair, a toaster oven, and more. After the folks at the table finished sharing, Rebecca pointed out to them that three out of every four of their personal stories involved consulting a digital source. The people in the room were also shoppers. The people in the room were also using digital channels in their shopping. While Rebecca was able to get senior executives to think like shoppers for a moment this time, she knew she wasn't going to truly get anywhere if every meeting started off with this much resistance and denial. She needed a bigger story to tell.

Rebecca's anthropological training taught her that the *way* you gather information can drive the story just as much as *what* information you are collecting. She took a hard look at the traditional research methods being used around her and came to believe that they were no longer working. With that, she wanted to wholly reinvent the way we asked people about shopping.

For her, the heart of the issue was Brand Narcissism. Surveys were being written from the point of view of the marketing executive who wanted to demonstrate that his latest campaign worked. These surveys read like needy, narcissistic dates who only cared about themselves. *Have you heard of me? What do you know about me? What do you think of me compared to your other dates? Am I your best date? Will we date again?* It was maddening to try to extract meaningful data from these old methods because they did not reflect a shopper's actual experience. When was the last time you were considering a brand of shampoo and thought, "*Well, this one is trustworthy, but that one offers good value for the money.*" You never have! Shoppers don't think that way, but all of the tools being used to understand them at the time assumed that they did.

Rebecca wanted to know what shoppers' needs were. How were they prioritizing those needs? How were they finding solutions to fit those needs? And did those solutions (the products they bought) succeed in their intended mission? So, she struck out on her own to demonstrate that things could and *should* be done differently.

At this point, Devora was working at the IPG Emerging Media Lab. The Lab was a kind of think tank for its global holding company where all kinds of folks in the media and advertising industry would come through to discuss new media channels and their impact on advertising decisions. The Lab served a broad range of CEOs and marketing leaders from quickserve giants to hardware companies and even global toy brands, among others. At the time, the Lab was situated in an office complex in the Mid-Wilshire area of Los Angeles where Ryan Seacrest produced his morning show and the Kardashians could often be seen coming through the lobby, entourage in tow. The Lab was on the fourth floor of a media agency that mostly held rows and rows of young media buyers pounding away at Excel files to buy their clients advertising spots across TV, radio, print, and out of home. This is what we now call "traditional media." Within this environment, there was a push to help clients understand the changes taking place towards the end of the aughts. Mobile phones were now emerging as a dominant force, but it was early yet: only 11 million of us had iPhones in 2008. And cord cutters had begun searching for content outside of traditional cable packages with services like Roku. Advertising leaders were nervous about what the future of their golden goose of TV buying would look like if media became a world with endless choice and fragmentation (hint—it did). The Lab was set up like a cozy (if clichéd) house of the future; we had a kitchen with a TV in the fridge door, a teenager's bedroom environment with gaming consoles, a connected living room with smart TVs, out of home-style screens that could read the faces of the audiences watching them, and even a retail store environment where we could show off advances in augmented reality, smart tags, and, of course, this was packed with more screens! It was an advertiser's wonderland.

Devora's job working at the Lab was to provide agency and client executives with a deeper understanding of the emerging media space and how it impacted their ability to reach their audiences effectively. Devora had learned how to balance a fun presentation with just enough data to bring the execs to the edge of their seats without causing a panic attack. Because it turns out, everything was at stake. The entire way their brand had established and funded their marketing initiatives, what it means to be a brand, how to generate awareness in a world of unending fragmentation among audiences, how ad agencies make money—all of this was starting to come crashing down, just as tech companies like Google and Facebook were ascending. To give you a sense of the shift we're talking about, in 2008 the Interactive Advertising Bureau and consulting giant PricewaterhouseCoopers estimated that online ad spending stood at $23.4 billion, or 17 percent of Nielsen's estimates of total ad spend for that year (Interactive Advertising Bureau, 2009) (Nielsen, 2009). Thirteen years later in 2021, Statista estimated the internet accounted for more than 50 percent of total ad revenue. Google's revenue for 2005 was $6.139 billion. By 2020 it had grown to *$169.478 billion*, not including its newer cloud services. Meaning that Google's business revenues rose by 2,660 percent over the 15-year period (yes, we wish we had bought stock then, too) (Securities and Exchange Commission, 2006, 2021). So, fortunes were about to change dramatically, and most people weren't ready.

While we hadn't yet met, Devora was experiencing the same frustrations Rebecca had experienced—trying to convince marketing and ad executives to take emerging media seriously. She wrote a paper detailing how Barack

Obama had become the first emerging media candidate, adroitly handling the shifting landscape to be elected the first Black President of the United States. She wrote trends presentations with headlines such as "Content is king" and "Mobile is dead" (that was a kind of Gandalf-like dead that dies as its original state and comes back more powerful, in case you were wondering) and gave impassioned presentations at the CES tech industry trade show about the future of tablets and smart homes. Clients would nod their heads and pretend to look intrigued—but go straight back to their age-old media plan. Maybe they'd throw a bone at the social media intern and let them create a Facebook page. Or maybe they'd make an app. Or throw a little money at search and banner ads. But they weren't convinced that online digital advertising was about to remake our world.

The brands that would consult with Devora were more worried about how they were losing control of the information their brand was putting out there. They weren't yet convinced that they would need to participate meaningfully in the world of customer reviews, blogs, or social media; they just wanted to *control* the conversations happening across them (insert very long and very loud, slightly evil cackle)... *as if!* Still, Devora and her colleagues put together countless workshops to help brands begin to understand that social media required new skills, new eyes, and a new acceptance of the democratization of content creation by users—including content about their brands, over which they had little control.

In 2009, the cosmos aligned and we met. Mutual contacts made the introduction. Kristin Luck, a serial entrepreneur in the research space, knew of Rebecca's desire to do something revolutionary and different. Kristin had heard of Devora at IPG, knew she was seeking out research support, and thought it would be a good fit. Little did Kristin realize she'd kick off a partnership that would change the way brands understood the role of digital in shopping. We connected instantly over this shared passion: clients were asking the wrong things and looking at the wrong data. Devora knew what she wanted to do, but had been met by resistance from other researchers. She was looking for a collaborator and she found one in Rebecca, who understood that traditional research approaches were flawed. Rebecca was ready to blow things up and try something risky. Devora, who knew exactly how to connect with these marketers and speak their language, was about to hand Rebecca the match. Because Devora wasn't a researcher, she didn't know that what she was about to ask Rebecca to do might not be possible. Or advisable! But they lit the fuse anyway.

Devora was a student of emerging media, not research. And Rebecca was a practitioner of research, not an expert in emerging media. We were two blind women who were trying to understand and validate how it appeared that online sources were flipping the script from the majority of decisions being made at shelf to the majority of decisions being made online. But anyone who knows either of us well knows that we really, *really* like being right. And we knew we were *right* about this. Now we had to figure out how to prove it to these executives who were comfortable with the old ways.

We realized early on this wasn't going to work if we tried to just tweak existing models. We had to put some research to work to show clients the impact online was having—or they'd fail, and we'd fail trying to convince them.

It might seem like this should have been an obvious solution. Talk to a bunch of people who just bought something to find out what caused them to buy it. It turns out it was kind of a revelation, for a few reasons. The first is that most brands and retailers did *consumer* research: *Do you like how this tastes? What color would you like better? What model do you prefer?* But hardly anyone was asking people who were in the process of *deciding* what that decision process was like. Another problem was that for clients who were researching the impact of media on purchase decisions, traditional research was very siloed—it would measure the impact of a TV ad, or optimize a print ad. So the first problem was that research was separating the answers by media type. And the second major problem was that it was still primarily built around broadcast media: TV, radio, print, out of home, and direct mail. Traditional research methodologies were built to evaluate traditional media. Online had been duct-taped into those models, but the data coming out of that research minimized the eruption that digital media was about to make in the world of shopping.

Getting Our First Shot

Devora was working with the IPG Lab President, John Ross. John had been the Chief Marketing Officer of home construction retailer Home Depot where he'd overseen one of the largest ad budgets in the world. He'd recently taken over the Lab by writing a Jerry Maguire-style manifesto which he'd sent to all four of the world's largest ad holding companies with the general theme being: *You run the largest media budgets in the world, but you have no idea how the people who buy stuff actually make decisions. You throw millions and even billions of dollars away each year on your glossy TV and print ads. Then you leave the trail cold when they arrive at the store.* One global ad agency head agreed and hired John to come run the Lab. What John wanted to know, and what he drove Devora and the team there to understand, was: *Does any of it matter to shoppers when making a decision? What information, what content do they actually need? And critically—how do they go from undecided to decided?* John brought a passion for research, but not traditional research. He'd started his own research practice that resembled more "man on the street" interviews than market research. By connecting with his customers at shelf, he'd learned how powerful intercepting shoppers *in active, decision-making mode* could be.

Because Devora had no prior research experience, she didn't give Rebecca the resistance that other clients might have. She was game for anything. For Devora and John, Rebecca was the eager collaborator they had been searching for. So we rolled up our sleeves and said, *Ok, how do we prove what's happening with the shift to digital? What are all the sources that are often ignored but are increasingly impacting people's choices?* We began by writing them all down, and it was an exhaustive list.

Once we got into the weeds, we started to build out a new kind of research tool. If we are going to ask people about their shopping decisions, how would folks remember what they had done when buying something six months ago? Oh, ok, we've got to talk to Recent Purchasers. Like, really recent. But what if they used a source but it didn't actually influence their decision? Now, we have to separate whether they used it from whether it was influential. At every step of the way we had to think about this methodology from the point of view of the shopper. That meant removing the Brand Narcissism perspective. Rather than asking about brands they knew or about brands whose products they bought, we started with what the shopper did. Instead of asking about brand attributes like "trustworthy" and "value for money," we asked about their reasons for purchase. The focus was on their experience, their needs, and their solutions to those needs (i.e. what they bought and why). Hours, weekends, evenings, and even holidays faded into the distance as we built this new methodology from thin air.

In this process, we began to coalesce around the idea of a metric that went beyond usage and incorporated influence. Later, we'll discuss how we developed Net Influence and the huge role it played in our research. We wanted some kind of measure that would allow us to gauge the importance of each source. Regardless of how much ad budget it had, or whether it was a traditional media source or in-store source. At the time (and even today, really) it was rare to put in-store sources on the continuum side by side with other media types. Because in-store wasn't a media advertising agencies could buy, most brands didn't think of it as a lever in the same way they did TV or radio. It just wasn't on their radar, and the ad industry had dismissed things with low visibility. But our hypothesis was that sources that were used by a minority of shoppers could still have a dramatic impact on shopping decisions *for those who used them* and should not be discounted.

We were looking at things from the shopper's view—and shoppers have never made the kinds of distinctions that marketers make. Shoppers use the information sources that are accessible and useful to them. They don't care which part of the marketing budget it sits in, just that it makes them smarter and more confident about their decisions. So we allowed ourselves to think like shoppers as we created this tool. The result of this iterative process was a methodology that could be nimble, yet comprehensive. It was entirely focused on the experience from the shopper's point of view.

What emerged from this process was a methodology that broke many traditional rules of research. Rebecca knew that if she'd tried to do this at her previous job, she would have encountered a lot of resistance. The freedom to build something so different was exhilarating and Devora shared the enthusiasm of finally seeing her and John's ideas on paper fully realized.

To start with, we didn't capture core audiences as defined by the brands. We wanted to talk to people who had actually bought the item and we wanted to talk to them as close as possible to the date of purchase. For grocery consumer packaged goods, this was the last 24 hours. For automotive, it might look more like three months depending on the balance of budget versus sample size. Whether that shopper fit a client's target segment was less important. We wanted to speak with Purchasers who remembered the experience. Next, we needed very large sample sizes. There were so many ways we wanted to cut the data: purchase channel (online vs. in-store), retailer brand, impulse vs. considered buys, and more. To get the most out of this research, we had to have robust base sizes that allowed us to dig into these groups.

Critically, our survey was based completely around a unique timeline chosen by the respondent—how long it took them to go from undecided to purchase. This meant every respondent had a unique data set that needed to be realigned in order to look at the results in aggregate. The research also had long lists of potential information sources that the respondents had to revisit multiple times—usage, influence, timeline, and content. Even today, when we share this methodology with clients there will invariably be a trained researcher in the room who will be taken aback by the approach. But from a shopper's point of view? Well, this is how they think about their "journey." This is how they organize their information and taking this survey was not only easy, but logical for them.

We began plotting more than 40 sources along a timeline, creating a heat map visual of when each source became a strong focal point for shoppers. Combining these usage maps with Net Influence gave clients a clear, visual representation of the impact these different sources can have on the shopper experience. For our clients, many of these heat maps became a revelation that would change the way they approached marketing.

In our first year, we studied a dozen or so categories—premium ham, payday loans, apparel, golf clubs, toilets, sinks, faucets, and quickserve restaurants. These early categories weren't sexy, but they shared something in common. They were in verticals with pragmatic marketers who had learned that, by addressing shopper needs, they could drive purchase. It made sense they were our early buyers of this research.

Ultimately, what was our key question?

Tell us what you did and how influential it was from the moment you decided to enter the category until the moment you bought.

This might not seem like a radical question. But 10 years ago marketers were still thinking not only about traditional media, but also about a very traditional path to purchase. Consultants were still presenting perky PowerPoint slides with models showing a linear path that started with what was known as the "First Moment of Truth" (we'll get to that in just a moment) and then went to awareness, consideration, and, ultimately, loyalty.

In fairness, this model worked well in a world that was constrained by consistent, known entities. When distribution chains and supplies were tightly controlled and it was hard for new and emerging brands to break in. When media channels were not unlimited and brands could drive large-scale awareness with flashy, expensive ad campaigns. When the seller knew more than the buyer and was, therefore, in control of the information and the shopping experience. For more than fifty years, virtually all shopping had happened in the retail environment and TV dominated the media landscape. By the end of the 1990s, this pleasant and somewhat stable retail and media environment was starting to show deep cracks.

Then, in the early 2000s, Procter & Gamble came up with a new framework that hypothesized that 70 percent of shopper decisions were made at shelf within seconds of noticing an item on the shelf. They called this "The First Moment of Truth" (Nelson and Ellison, 2005). The First Moment of Truth (FMOT) created the shopper marketing industry as we know it today. It gave brands and retailers a common language to use when thinking about shoppers, standing in the aisle and considering the choices in front of them. It also helped both brands and advertisers develop a new toolkit of in-store advertising with which they could target shoppers. P&G created a head of FMOT, opened FMOT offices and created a whole new world of in-store marketing. It was part of then-CEO A. G. Lafley's "The consumer is boss" mantra (Buckley, 2005). The company integrated it into everything, going so far as to engineer the entire supply chain to work backwards from it (Supply Chain Brain, 2006). In large part, FMOT was an early reaction to the fragmentation that had begun—it gave brands another way to reach shoppers now that there were more than 24 channels on TV or a core group of print publications that everyone was reading.

The problem was that, just a few years later, the First Moment of Truth was no longer supported by the data. So what was happening? How, in just a few years, had decision making gone from primarily happening at shelf to occurring largely before the shopper arrived at the store?

The answer was simple: online.

Online was not just another media channel; online was a *whole galaxy* of owned, earned, and paid media with both brand and consumer narratives, and it was evolving rapidly. The traditional research tools of the past that had measured broadcast media in the same way for the last half century or more were not going to capture the story of what was happening. Bringing all of these ideas together led us to the concept of "pre-shopping." Up until this point, marketers thought of shopping as something that happened at the shelf, but we had come to realize most consumers had already been "shopping" in some form before ever walking into the store.

Let's show you what we mean. Take this heat map (Figure 1.1). This was an early method we used to express to clients the way in which influence was shifting from traditional media to digital media.

On the Y axis is influence. On the X axis is time from purchase. And the brightness of the heat is the number of shoppers who said they used a particular source prior to purchase. You can see that while the greatest influence was happening a few moments before purchase, there are bright blooms showing influence occurring as many as two to three months prior to purchase.

FIGURE 1.1   Heat map displaying influence and timing of in-store Source Usage

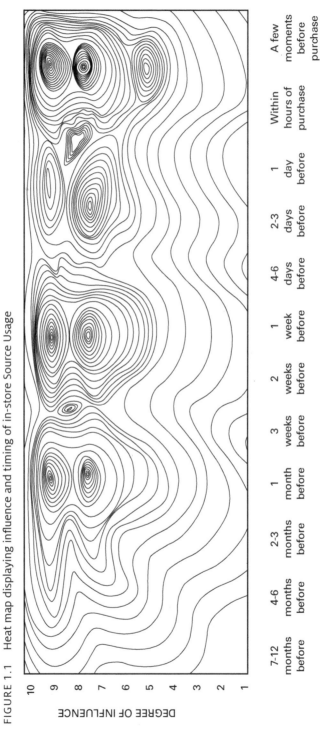

Over the last decade since we began this research, the sources available have expanded, with traditional media joined by podcasts, online retail media, TikTok, and others. And our Source Usage list has stayed current with the options available today. When we would show this list to clients, they never believed we'd see any level of influence from digital and social sources. They also frequently discounted the influence of the retail store. They were raised in a world where TV was the driving force of awareness and consideration—and in many ways, while the ad agencies wanted to have a piece of the digital media pie, they were between a rock and a hard place because, ultimately, TV paid the bills.

These heat maps were mostly theater. But they served an important purpose—revealing that the traditional path to purchase funnel was dead. Again and again, the heat maps showed that influence was taking place at far different times, places, and ways than brand marketers expected. Sometimes influence was happening months before a brand had anticipated. Or sometimes days or weeks later than they suspected. We often pointed to an example that Devora wrote about in her book with John Ross, *Fire in the Zoo*, regarding the curious ways in which people shop for boxed cake mix. In the case of a cake mix, one would assume that influence would take place at shelf, or maybe a day or two at most in advance. But the cake mix findings revealed that influence was taking place several days out from purchase. How could that be? How could people possibly spend four to six days thinking about a $2 purchase? What our research revealed is that it wasn't the price of the cake mix that represented the consumer's real risk. It was the risk of getting their kid's birthday celebration wrong. Four to six days seems like a lot if you think about the purchase from the perspective of some pre-packaged cake mix in a cardboard box, often sold at a discount. But four to six days considering your options—looking online for recipes, asking friends for suggestions via social media, re-reading the back of the box, asking your child what they want—is nothing when it's your only kid's fifth birthday party and you don't want to fail.

In a way, the heat maps were a metaphor for what we were attempting to do. By combining usage, influence, and time, they revealed more than just the shopper journey. They were a proxy for the shopper brain. Similar to the brain, the shopper journey could start a thought, take a turn, decide against it, go back, circle around, and do a few zig-zags and jumping jacks, have a panic attack, calm down, do some research, and then finally get to a place where the shopper felt they were ready to purchase. The neural-like lines of the heat maps continually reminded us that this wasn't about trying to nail down a path that marketers could just learn and repeat ad nauseum—but instead, accepting that it was a wild, ever-changing, dynamic journey that demanded new thinking, new research, and a new language.

We would often play a game where we'd ask our clients to guess what the journey would look like—how long did it take shoppers to go from undecided to decided? What sources were most used by shoppers? Which sources might have lower usage but higher influence on decision making? In subsequent chapters we'll come back more to this specific framework and how we are adapting it for brand marketers 15 years on—but for now, suffice to say, we and our clients were often wrong about when, where, and how influence was taking place.

Our Baby Named ZMOT

In 2010, our team met with Jim Lecinski and Google. Jim's team had been seeing similar trends in their data for a while; what we had blandly called "pre-shopping" they had brilliantly conceptualized as the "Zero Moment of Truth." They had been presenting their findings to CMOs, but they wanted to validate their data with insights from shoppers. Jim was a VP of Sales at Google who was responsible for supporting leading companies across a range of verticals, including CPG, health and beauty, travel, automotive, apparel, and tech. He wanted to apply our research to help him convince marketers in these categories to shift their dollars to digital.

It's hard to believe that now, in the era of Big Tech where Google was valued at $1.4 *trillion* in 2021, that there was a time when it had to work for ad dollars. That as a sales guy at Google you'd have to create a slide presentation and *convince* people to spend money with you. But it's true. Google was already in a huge growth phase, but without unlocking more ad dollars that were locked up in traditional media, it would be hard to grow in the way they wanted to. Jim was responsible for engaging large customers— Fortune 500s, the Global 2000—to spend more on Google. Jim had started there in 2005 when ecommerce sales were in the low, low single digits, only 2.6 percent of total US retail sales in Q4 of 2005 according to the US Census Bureau.

Jim would show up with his sales directors and say, *Hey, we're seeing in our data that people are actually searching in your category*—for laundry detergent, home goods, or financial services. But the clients would insist based on their gut or the prevailing wisdom at the time, "they're not searching for my stuff." This refrain was followed by, "*Nobody uses the internet to comparison-shop cruises, nobody uses the internet to comparison-shop life insurance, nobody uses the internet to comparison-shop olive oil.*"

And Jim would say, "*Well, what do you think they're searching for?*" And the clients would hem and haw and say any other category but their own. And despite having the Google data underpinning Jim's pitch, the clients weren't buying his argument—or his search ads—in the ways (and at the rates) that Google wanted.

So Jim hired the team at the Lab to apply our research methodology to vet his hypothesis and put it to work for Google. We started with 5,000 shoppers across 12 categories, and later another 7,500 interviews across another 15 categories. We later used the data to help Jim write his eBook, ZMOT (Google, 2011).

The shopper study with Google was a neat opportunity because seeing influence play out across a wide range of categories was revelatory.

We learned that two-thirds of shoppers in most categories were relying on a digital or online (ZMOT) source before purchasing (Google, 2011). We also learned that shoppers were becoming increasingly savvy about bringing different sources of information together to inform their buying decisions. They'd do a search, read a review, look at a brand or retail website, go to the store and talk with an associate, then compare prices at the shelf. On average, shoppers were using more than 10 sources of information before making a purchase decision. It makes sense that the number of sources used would be high for automotive or electronics purchases—but we saw that even for categories such as makeup or pain relievers, it was more than six sources. Some less confident clients might have thought, *Well, search is only at 30 percent of usage for health and beauty.* But, early on, Google flipped the script and said, *30 percent?! It might not be the 80 percent of search used when buying a car, but who cares? If 30 percent of shoppers are now using online for regular, fast moving goods purchases under $10, we're moving into a different universe.* And they were right.

Above all, the key thing that we were learning was that shoppers were *hungry for information.* And this meant that there was no longer such a thing as a "low engagement category." Now, because there was no limit to what you could learn from a quick search on your laptop or smartphone, every category was up for consideration and scrutiny. Author Daniel Pink calls this the transformative shift from "information asymmetry to information parity" (Pink, 2013).

Needless to say, this makes marketers' jobs much harder. Now every marketer, whether they're selling a $5 hair clip or a $50,000 car, has to think about how to create content that will satisfy shoppers' questions, concerns, and voracious appetite to *know more*. Our research showed this shift in one clear metric: the number one thing shoppers look for from brands. For years, the number one thing shoppers wanted from brands was *value*. Today, it's the *information* to help make a smarter decision. In some ways, providing helpful information has actually become a form of value to shoppers.

Jim likens it to the fancy word that means people who like wine: "oenophiles." He says marketers must acknowledge "the oenophilification of every category" where everyone has become the equivalent of an amateur sommelier. As Jim says, "it's now that for every freaking category. Now, there's mustard that's like that." We couldn't agree more. This "oenophilification of every category", as Jim so succinctly puts it, is at the heart of how the shopper journey has changed.

Between the work we were doing together for brands and the findings from the ZMOT study, we now knew two new, immutable truths that would stay with us for good:

- One, there was no linear path. Shoppers were entering at different points, their journeys were wildly different in terms of length and intensity, sources would often be revisited. Not a linear path and more of a spiral narrowing their choices down by revisiting and honing their research until they made a decision.

- And two, every category could be a high consideration category with experts and minutia being studied and reported on. There are paper plates now made from avocado pits for the environmentally conscious consumer. So yes—it applies to every category and every brand on the planet.

ZMOT had a massive impact on the industry. It turns out, we were really on to something. As Jim says, in hindsight the research "took on a greater life, and we stopped counting at 300,000 reads of the book. It got far more traction than we ever imagined."

Although it began as a business-to-business (B2B) sales exercise for Google, what it accomplished was much bigger. ZMOT proved that online marketing was essential for any brand. Not just essential to search, but the whole layered lasagna of the online ecosystem—blogs, reviews, social media, online video, listicles, forums, online ratings, and everything else. And these sources were working together with traditional media sources to help shoppers form opinions about the products and brands they would ultimately buy.

For us, ZMOT launched our careers. Devora became a researcher out of it and Rebecca's company became known for its shopper and tech expertise, working for the likes of eBay, Hyundai, Snapchat, YouTube, and Viking Cruises. But the magical understanding it left us with was the framework of using usage and influence as key metrics for tracking and revealing the shopper journey from a quantitative perspective:

Where do shoppers go for information? And how influential are each of those sources?

We still love tracking how usage rises or falls in different categories—and for different brands and different channels. To this day, if you want to have an entertaining conversation, get us over a beer to start talking about how usage and influence can change radically by category, demographic, and psychographic. For example, we've found that dads consistently use more sources than moms before making a purchase. Millennials appear to be particularly anxious when shopping and typically do more research than other generations. Premium water buyers are positively addicted to learning more about their purchase (because, again, they aren't buying *water*; they're buying *recovery* from their workout). For years, consumer reviews were one of the most widely used and highly influential sources. Then, about two years ago, they started to fall off a bit. They're still important, but shoppers know the game is rigged and have become less trusting of consumer reviews as a key shopper information source. They check them out, but they use other means to inform their final decision. Another example: podcasts. We had podcasts on our usage chart for years and it hung out in the bottom left corner of every quadrant chart with the dust bunnies and print magazines. Low usage. Low influence. Then, we started seeing it get a little higher influence. And then one day, there it was, in the upper left quadrant—high influence and used by 30 percent of shoppers. We saw a similar trend with Facebook; for years it was low usage, low influence, then briefly it was low usage but high influence. And then one day, probably about the time it hit over 1 billion users, it fell into the bottom right quadrant alongside print and traditional media sources—high usage, low influence. Despite its in-depth targeting capabilities and ability to command ad dollars, it had jumped the shark in a way—in the minds of shoppers at any rate.

These concepts, *usage and influence*, have remained a foundational element of our approach to understanding the shopper journey and shopper brain. Since the creation of ZMOT, we have continued to evolve and stretch our methodology and thinking. Over the course of this book, we will take you through our data and what those insights mean for researchers and marketers. Before we can begin that, we need to set the context for this conversation by understanding the current state of consumer insights and how we got here.

KEY TAKEAWAYS

- The digital age has completely transformed how people approach their shopping. They leaned into ecommerce and online research heavily, but the advertising industry was slow to adapt.

- We always need to challenge our assumptions about what consumers are doing and where they are going for information, or someone else will.

- The key to understanding where you need to meet your shoppers lies in understanding how shoppers use sources to find information.

References

Associated Press (2013) Number of active users at Facebook over the years, Yahoo News, May 1. https://news.yahoo.com/number-active-users-facebook-over-230449748.html (archived at https://perma.cc/T6L6-WP6X)

Berlin, L (2008) Lessons of Survival, from the dot-com attic, *The New York Times*, November 23. www.nytimes.com/2008/11/23/business/23proto.html (archived at https://perma.cc/95AB-TA5P)

Buckley, N (2005) The power of original thinking, *Financial Times*, January 13. www.ft.com/content/0193a5b0-658e-11d9-8ff0-00000e2511c8 (archived at https://perma.cc/47VN-KAF9)

Google (2011) *Winning the Zero Moment of Truth*. www.thinkwithgoogle.com/future-of-marketing/emerging-technology/2011-winning-zmot-ebook/ (archived at https://perma.cc/RC4P-Q2NG)

Interactive Advertising Bureau (2009) *IAB Internet Advertising Revenue Report: 2008 full-year results*. www.iab.com/wp-content/uploads/2015/05/IAB_PwC_2008_full_year.pdf (archived at https://perma.cc/C7DK-F9HS)

MacroTrends (2021) Amazon Revenue 2006–2021, MacroTrends, ND. www.macrotrends.net/stocks/charts/AMZN/amazon/revenue (archived at https://perma.cc/CQ53-8SGE)

Nelson, E and Ellison, S (2005) In a shift, marketers beef up ad spending inside stores, *Wall Street Journal*, September 21. www.wsj.com/articles/SB112725891535046751 (archived at https://perma.cc/TRL6-VDVP)

Nielsen (2009) US ad spending fell 2.6% in 2008, Nielsen reports, press release, March 13. www.nielsen.com/wp-content/uploads/sites/3/2019/04/nielsen2008adspend-release.pdf (archived at https://perma.cc/N4ZS-DLZ5)

Pink, D H (2013) *To Sell Is Human: The surprising truth about moving others*, Riverhead Books, New York

Ross, J and Rogers, D (2018) *Fire in the Zoo: A book about shopper influence, marketing mania, retailer chaos, advertising pitfalls, consumer confidence, converting customers and how screaming at people usually doesn't work*, CreateSpace Independent Publishing Platform

Securities and Exchange Commission (2006) Google announces fourth quarter and fiscal year 2005 results, press release, January 31. www.sec.gov/Archives/edgar/data/1288776/000119312506016138/dex991.htm (archived at https://perma.cc/3NY2-HLMV)

Securities and Exchange Commission (2021) Alphabet announces fourth quarter and fiscal year 2020 results, press release, February 2. www.sec.gov/Archives/edgar/data/0001652044/000165204421000006/googexhibit991q420.htm (archived at https://perma.cc/4CDA-KYLN)

Statista (2021) Global ad spend distribution 2020, by medium, Statista, ND. www.statista.com/statistics/376260/global-ad-spend-distribution-by-medium/ (archived at https://perma.cc/G6AL-4RD9)

Supply Chain Brain (2006) Procter & Gamble uses consumer demand info to drive supply network, February 1. www.supplychainbrain.com/articles/575-procter-gamble-uses-consumer-demand-info-to-drive-supply-network (archived at https://perma.cc/8VAY-9J2Z)

US Census Bureau (2021) Estimated quarterly US retail sales (adjusted): Total and e-commerce. www.census.gov/retail/index.html (archived at https://perma.cc/MX3S-36M9)

0 2

The Hidden Danger of Brand Narcissism

Have you ever taken a survey and thought to yourself, "*Well, that depends…*" when you try to answer a question? That indecisiveness came not because you couldn't make up your mind, but because you were being asked a question that has no answer. A good question that yields a good answer is written from the point of view of the person being asked, not the person doing the asking. It is much easier to answer the question "*Are you happy with this product?*" than it is to answer the question "*How likely are you to buy this product in the future?*" Well, that depends… Much has been written about implicit bias in educational testing, policing, or medical responsiveness. The same concepts apply to the market research industry. While we certainly have our socioeconomic biases to attend to, we also have a much more serious problem. Market research is rooted in Brand Narcissism.

Consider the questions above. Marketers want to know if people are going to buy their product in the future. (Even better if they buy that product after seeing an ad.) The answer "very likely" to the question of "*How likely are you to buy this product in the future?*" justifies their company's marketing expenditures, predicts growth, and supports the need to increase budgets. Like Narcissus gazing at his reflection, market researchers ask questions from their point of view, as if the consumer is their mirror reflection. But consumers aren't like researchers, and their opinions on products are the ones that actually matter.

The ugly truth behind the number of people that answer "very likely" is that many of them very likely qualified their answers in their head. *Very likely, but that depends*. But on what? A future that is unpredictable—innovations, disruptions, economic downturns, personal fortunes—so much of what goes into that answer is unknown. Yet, we see 48 percent of people are "very likely" to buy our product, so we go buy a round of drinks for the marketing team for delivering a great success. This scenario is exactly how Brand Narcissism creates misleading and potentially damaging "stories" about consumer perceptions. Those stories make sense to a researcher who isn't looking outward for the real thing—those consumers answered questions just like the brand would have, so they must be right.

We aren't saying that market research companies are illogical or vain or irresponsible. Not at all. There is a history to how we got here and, like many histories, it was formed by very smart people making very smart decisions at a specific time. But as the world evolves, those decisions no longer hold up. We know more now about how people think than ever before and any neuroscientist would tell you we have so much more to learn. The intent of this book is not to dismiss the real value of the market research industry. Rather, we want to take a step back and understand how we got into this tangle. And, hopefully, figure out how to stop staring at our own reflection to provide a clearer picture.

Questioning the Questions

A decade into her market research career, Rebecca was convinced that Brand Narcissism in research was giving brands all the wrong information. With a century-old multi-billion dollar industry, it would be logical to think that the best practices are time-tested, reliable, stable, and entirely understood. As Rebecca was transitioning from graduate school research in primatology to a career in market research, she entered the profession with a clear understanding of the importance of methodology and statistical rigor—principles that translated easily to her new career. However, as an anthropologist, Rebecca was also keenly aware of the bias that observers can bring into their work. Whether they are studying non-human primates, other cultures, or consumers, researchers have a tendency to bring themselves into the mix and shift the focus away from what's most valuable.

Margaret D. LeCompte's groundbreaking 1987 paper, "Bias in the biography," broke open the conversation in anthropology about the inherent biases in the researcher that inform and influence their observations. Every human has biases, developed from infancy, which originate in their culture, socioeconomic status, and myriad other factors. LeCompte argued, rightfully, that these biases cannot be eliminated. It's impossible for a human to observe without putting those observations into a context that makes sense to them. What we must do, instead, is openly address those biases by acknowledging they exist, naming what they are, and recognizing how they might be framing our observations into a different context.

Rebecca's undergraduate thesis directly targeted a traditional, biased assumption about mating in non-human primates. Most primatologists, before the era of Jane Goodall, Diane Fossey, and Birute Galdikas, were men observing mating behaviors and hypothesizing the reasons for the behavior they were seeing. To those male researchers, the aggressive male monkeys seemed to dominate the reproductive playing field—mating more frequently than less robust males and, therefore, propagating the gene pool with future aggressive males. Men, looking for their own reflection, focused on the males.

However, Rebecca's work with John D. Berard in 1993 at the Caribbean Primate Research Center in Cayo Santiago clearly defied those assumptions. Rebecca studied mating behavior in rhesus macaques. John's unique technique of following one female for a full day provided a much richer insight into the complex social dynamics affecting mating behavior. Rather than focusing on the group at large and seeing what was happening out in the open, following one female meant researchers were often being led away to secret hiding spots and quiet spaces far away from the main group. What they found there were younger, less aggressive males with lower social status waiting patiently for the female to arrive.

If these meetings were pre-arranged or if they were simply happenstance will never really be understood. But what was clear was that the females were actively choosing to mate with males of lower social status, some from different groups, at great risk to themselves. If and when they were discovered, the dominant males would always attack the females. Yet, these females continued to make these clandestine appointments. By *changing the methodology*, John had revealed an entire new world of behavior that had been missed by traditional observation. This was a lesson that fundamentally transformed how Rebecca looks at research and behavior. There's always another side of the story, if only we decide to look with a different lens and away from our reflection.

So, ten years into her career, frustrated with Brand Narcissism, Rebecca decided she needed to revisit the methodology. *No one seemed to be questioning the questions.* Maybe that was the root of the problem.

Market Research Origins

To understand how we got here, we have to first take a step back and look at the evolution of market research. There are excellent reasons why we find ourselves asking about awareness, familiarity, and consideration, but they originated in now outdated models. Those models are being tweaked to account for changes in shopping, but they need to be completely rethought from the ground up. While there are textbooks that go into much greater detail about the history of market research, what we are presenting here is an overview, from our perspective, illustrating how Brand Narcissism became the norm.

Marketers have always tried to organize the world of shopping into a framework that feels both philosophically rational and empirically definable. People manage the enormous amount of input they receive every second through an elaborate system of categorization and modeling. Malcolm Gladwell's *Blink* (2005) talked about this extensively. Daniel Kahneman's *Thinking, Fast and Slow* (2013) revolutionized the way we think about behavior by breaking thinking into two distinct operations—System 1, which is nearly automatic; and System 2, which is more analytical. There has been a ton of research to illustrate that we need to make rapid decisions about the world around us. To process all that information quickly, our brains organize data into patterns. Without these patterns and models, we'd meet every situation completely fresh. Imagine hearing your cell phone ring and having to learn each time that the noise coming out of the phone means you have a call coming in.

These organizational models allow us to do things like drive safely while our minds are occupied with other thoughts. They allow us to function in the world and make smart decisions based on the information we've learned over our lifetime.

This predisposition towards patterns also surfaces in how we philosophically organize the world, allowing us to make sense of things. Take something as simple as brushing your teeth. We have the stories that people have told us since a young age about the importance of dental hygiene. And, importantly, we have empirical evidence to support those stories. The painful experience of discovering swollen gums at the dentist is a powerful reminder to floss more often. Plus, we have data from scientists and medical professionals supporting this practice. Because of all these inputs, we mechanically brush our teeth as part of our daily routine. Skipping a day feels uncomfortable, not only because of the unclean sensation in your mouth, but also because we know we are bucking a known, proven practice.

These models also show up in business and the way we organize our roles and responsibilities. Since the emergence of mass retail in the early 1900s with mail order catalogues and chain retail stores, marketers have organized the world of shopping into a framework that feels both philosophically rational and empirically definable. These models help characterize how market research evolved. The industry began in the early 1910s with Claude Hopkins, who studied the impact of different ads in mail order catalogues and print publications. Based on the mail-in orders, early marketers could determine which advertisements and messaging performed the best. While this offered empirical evidence, the method didn't put the results into a philosophical context: Why did that one ad outperform the other?

In the 1920s, Daniel Starch developed the first "framework" for advertising and marketers. He postulated that there was a structured way in which advertising was consumed by people. First the ad had to be seen. Then, the consumer had to read the ad. Next, they needed to believe the content of the ad. From there, the consumer had to remember the ad so the next time they were in the category to purchase, they would remember it. Lastly, they had to act through purchase.

What was revolutionary about Starch's model was that it broke out the steps of advertising effectiveness into measurable pieces:

- Awareness: People have to be exposed to the ad. Did they see it?
- Stopping power: The ad has to get their attention. Did they pay attention?
- Credibility: Snake oil salesmen are only as effective as they are convincing. Is your claim believable? Does it make a compelling argument?
- Retention: If an ad immediately leaves the consumer's mind, then all of the above steps were for naught. While it would be impossible for a consumer to remember all the details of an ad, they at least need to come away with a positive impression and a desire to learn more or to act through purchase. What did they remember about the ad?
- Purchase: The ultimate outcome of this model is to bring customers to the point of purchase. Did they end up buying the product?

It's clear why marketers fell in love with the approach. Not only was this measurable, but there were clear solutions. People didn't see the ad? Rethink your placement. It wasn't engaging? Create more compelling visuals. Not credible? Say "9 out of 10 agree." Don't remember it? Find a hook, like a jingle or snappy saying. Didn't purchase the product? Make it more attractive on the shelf.

While not every problem had a tidy solution, depending on the category and target consumer, this framework gave marketers a rationale for consumer behavior and a roadmap on how to sell more products.

The formal market research industry emerged from Starch's framework nearly overnight. At about the same time, George Gallup developed the concept of aided recall. Showing a person an ad and asking if they had seen it previously is a flawed methodology. People might be inclined to falsely say yes because they are being polite or don't want to look uniformed. Or, perhaps, the ad was similar to another they remember. Gallup's idea was to trigger memories of the ad without actually showing the ad to the respondent. By asking about the brand, the message, the visuals, and other aspects, Gallup was able to uncover "true recall."

The potent combination of Starch's framework and Gallup's evolution of accounting for human memory and psychology created a powerful point of view that still looms large over the market research industry today.

The Emergence of Consumer Choice

One important thing to note about the time period when market research was first launched was the limitations that consumers faced when considering what to buy. Unlike today, there were just a handful of brands to choose from back then. Additionally, national product distribution and retail chains were still emerging, meaning that consumers could have wildly different experiences at shelf in terms of what brands were available. A town without a mass retail chain could have completely different products available for their consumers.

Additionally, national brands with large distribution networks were still emerging. Coca-Cola, Sears, and Ford had huge name recognition and could reach most consumers, but many other brands were limited to regional areas of influence.

Consumers had limited choice. Mail order catalogues and brick-and-mortar stores were the primary options to get products. The products they could buy were limited by what was available at the store. Advertising was a piece of the puzzle but did not yet carry the weight it would in the decades to come. Distribution was still king. A brand that could get on every shelf would almost inevitably win.

Then, the brand explosion of the 1940s happened. All of a sudden, instead of a handful of brand choices, consumers started to see their supermarket and department store shelves crowded with variety. From dish detergent to garden soil to toasters, every category experienced a "gold rush" of new brands. This was due to several factors. First, technology was improving, allowing brands to come out with "new and improved" products or bring a unique feature to market. In the post-World War II era, money was flowing and challenger brands were encroaching into categories to get a piece of the market share.

Consumers had more choice than ever before, and this presented a new problem for marketers. The metrics of awareness, stopping power, credibility, and retention were no longer enough. Just putting your product in front of someone with believable claims was not driving purchase the way it used to. Consumers needed another reason to choose you. A point of differentiation. However, in most categories, brands were reaching a level of parity. Any new stain removal power or longer shelf-life could be trumped by a competitor in a year or less. Unless they wanted to race to the bottom on price, brands had to find a new way to stand out from the crowd.

The Rise of Brands and Brand Identity

While branding—the idea of creating a relatable, engaging personality for your company's products—had been in play for decades, it was taken up a notch in the 1950s and 1960s as brands strived to achieve the next highest goal—loyalty. It was no longer enough to get a consumer to purchase your product. You had to earn their loyalty and earn their next purchase. But how does a brand build loyalty in a crowded marketplace with relative product parity? By building a relationship and connection with the consumers. By creating an identity that resonates and inspires loyalty.

Bill Bernbach's famous "Think Small" campaign for Volkswagen is often lauded as the turning point for creativity in advertising in the 1960s. Volkswagen had an oddly designed, small car trying to break into the US marketplace dominated by General Motors, Chrysler, and Ford. Not only did the car look unusual, but it bucked the trend of "bigger is better" that US manufacturers were pursuing. An additional wrinkle was that World War II was not quite 20 years in the past, and supporting such a distinctly German company—one that historically had direct ties to the Nazi party—came with its own disadvantages. Given a seemingly insurmountable problem,

Bernbach took a truly emotional approach. He didn't talk about the car's features or legacy of quality. He didn't try to convince his audience that this car could compete with the US classics. Rather, he took a negative point, the size, and turned it into a point of honor and pride for the little car that could. He leaned into bucking the establishment, which was exactly the right tone to take in the early 1960s when then-young Boomers started chafing against that establishment.

Bernbach's ad didn't just boost sales for the brand. It transformed Volkswagen into a new kind of symbol. The brand meant something deeper and more personal than other cars. Volkswagen became synonymous with freedom, independence, and standing out on your own, and embraced the counterculture sentiment that would come to dominate the decade. This wasn't a car. It was an icon.

Once the power of that tactic started to sink in at ad agencies, everyone pivoted and began chasing the next "Think Small" idea. It's no coincidence that Apple would introduce itself 20 years later with their "Think Different" campaign that created an equally iconic identity. The echoes of Bernbach still resonate.

With all the ad agencies pursuing this new goal—building a brand that people wanted to commit to and not just buy—researchers realized they were missing out on a critical metric. Starch's model got them to purchase, but what happens after purchase? Should we start measuring the next thing the consumer does?

What emerged from this age was a new loyalty metric. Research agencies began adding to Starch's model and looking for new ways to capture this more elusive asset. Thinking around buying and what went into the process was also maturing. John Howard's work on buyer behavior applied more scientific methods taken from psychology and sociology to inform how to measure something like loyalty. His book with Jagdish Sheth, *The Theory of Buyer Behavior* (1969), became an academic lodestone and set the conversation around brand building and consumer engagement for decades to come. They describe how the shopper journey doesn't end at purchase. Rather, purchase and intention inform the buyer's satisfaction, which then informs that buyer's overall feelings towards a brand. This changes the future variables affecting future purchases, resulting in a kind of feedback loop. Shoppers who have good experiences with a brand will be more likely to buy from it again, absent an intervening exogenous variable.

By the 1990s, market research was a mature science and critical component of branding and advertising strategy. "Account Planner" titles were popping up in advertising agencies as "voice of the consumer" advocates who used research to represent the consumer in the boardroom. Global research companies like IPSOS, Nielsen, and Millward Brown had trained a generation of marketers and researchers to think of the customer path to purchase as a linear funnel from awareness to consideration to purchase to loyalty.

Measuring Persuasion, Involvement, and Salience

In the early 1990s, one of those scrappy Account Planners named Mike Hall, who was working at the agency Davies Riley Smith Maclay, had a lightning bolt moment in a bathtub and cracked a new solution for addressing advertising performance that expanded on and refined the traditional funnel. Rebecca began working at Mike's firm, Hall and Partners, in 2000 and he was already a legend in the industry. Mike added something new to the traditional ideas of credibility and memorability measures established by Starch so many decades ago. Mike added the ideas of persuasion, involvement, and salience. Today, these seem like no-brainer concepts, but at the time they had not been adequately measured in a quantitative way.

- Persuasion was simply whether or not the ad motivated a consumer to act. Did it make you more interested in the brand or the product? This was a softer metric than purchase intent. Respondents didn't have to commit to saying they would purchase and could talk instead about whether the ad "got them thinking." Advertisers loved this because it removed the requirement of ads directly impacting sales. They could finally start measuring what they felt was there all along—a cumulative effect of advertising wherein each ad and touchpoint layers onto the previous to build a brand relationship. Each ad did not have to directly tie to sales.

- Involvement took the research beyond stopping power to a more sophisticated measurement of connection. Ads can shout at consumers to grab eyeballs, but can those same ads hold on to the consumer? This measured how much consumers actually connected with the ad. This measure was also critically important for brand health tracking. Did consumers have a relationship with the brand that went above functional benefits?

- Salience was a completely new idea and does not have an analogous component in Starch's model. Salience was about standing out: a brand that has momentum is on its way up and something to take notice of. In the post-Bernbach world of advertising, it was a critical concept that had gone completely unmeasured. Salience was a combination of awareness, stopping power, credibility, and persuasion all rolled into one. If a brand was salient, they were more likely to be top of mind when consumers were choosing a brand to buy.

Mike's perspective took the ad agency by storm and his little research company turned into a global powerhouse within a decade. Mike's willingness to change the model and step away from the way things had always been done made a significant impact on Rebecca's approach to research, which ultimately led to connecting with Devora and creating ZMOT. Thanks, Mike!

Digital Media Changes the Shopper Journey

For most of the late 1990s and early 2000s, larger research companies were scrambling to adapt and update their models. With the onset of digital media and ecommerce, the industry began to feel a little like the Wild West after nearly a century of relative stability. Mike recognized this too and attempted to reform his model in the mid-2000s to accommodate the emergence of digital in the shopper journey experience. Like most successful people, he was trying to adapt those winning ideas. Unfortunately, they'd need more of a wholesale makeover.

People still needed to learn about products, they still needed compelling reasons to buy, and they would ultimately become loyal customers to a brand. Digital marketing and ecommerce were seen as niche add-ons to the existing way of seeing the world. No one knew we needed to rethink the entire shopper journey because no one understood yet how fundamentally the shopper journey would change. And, not just the journey, but the shopper mindset as well.

The assumption that digital media would act like a traditional broadcast channel was flawed from the beginning. The difference, and what an enormous difference it turned out to be, is that digital was being co-created by consumers at the same time. Even before websites let you review their products, consumers were creating their own review blogs and leaving feedback on message boards. They were starting to make how-to videos on YouTube and share their favorite products. Control of the narrative was shifting to the consumer.

One of Rebecca's favorite stories to tell clients is when she was going to buy her first car in 1998. Trudging through the early days of the brand websites and third party information, Rebecca had printed out details about every car she was interested in purchasing. Those specifications and reviews were then matched with dealer incentives, financing options, and data on resale value. This researcher was serious about making an informed decision! Rebecca's first stop was a Honda dealership. Their brand was well known for quality and reliability. She wanted a dependable and financially sound car. Armed with her binder full of print outs, Rebecca approached the salesman and started talking about what she wanted.

He was bemused and teased her about the binder, but listened patiently. Then Rebecca got to the incentives that were on offer and what she knew the dealer had paid for the car. At that point, the salesman started to get defensive and blustered about price. After a few tense minutes he said, "This is Honda. I don't have to negotiate." Rebecca walked away, but found the experience so frustrating that she's sworn to never own a Honda for the rest of her life.

Now, that's not a story about a plucky young researcher standing up to a big, bad car salesman. That's a story about a brand who had not yet pivoted to the new reality. Their buyers were going to come armed with information and they better train their staff on how to deal with it. But it isn't just about training staff on new techniques, is it? No, this would require, from Honda and everyone else, a fundamental rethinking of how they run their business—from dealer franchise management, to MSRP, to incentives, to salespeople. The whole infrastructure needed to adjust to the new reality.

As Clay Christensen talks about in his book *The Innovator's Dilemma* (2011), it can be very challenging for any brand that has been successful to see change coming and adapt to that change in enough time. Adjusting a large brand is like trying to turn a cruise ship. You need a lot of time and space to get it done.

In the early 2000s, brands would talk about consumers as co-creators, advocates, and fans. This was loyalty at its zenith. Getting a consumer to share their experience with a product, to recommend your brand, to truly co-create content was the ultimate measure of loyalty. In 2003, Bain & Company adopted Fred Reichheld's Net Promoter Score as a way to measure a new form of loyalty and it took off like a rocket (Bain & Company, 2021).

Brand Loyalty Measured: Net Promoter Score

Loyalty, until this point, had been thought of as likelihood to purchase again. A consumer with high or very high likelihood to buy the product again was considered loyal to the brand. However, just like the problem with Starch's framework stopping at purchasing, repeat purchasing didn't tell us enough about what the consumer would really do. That's because repeat purchase was not always a guarantee in a rapidly changing world. We'll get to that in a bit, but the problem with using "likelihood to purchase again" as a metric is that it assumes that the consumer is locked. That a loyal customer is just that—loyal, and nothing else. That's the end of their story. Brands and marketers want to focus on moving consumers through the funnel, from unaware to aware to consideration to purchase to loyalty. The focus was on increasing the size of the loyalty bucket and moving early funnel consumers closer towards loyalty. Matt Stefl, Clinical Professor Marketing and Co-Director of the M-School at Loyola Marymount University, agrees. "This idea of brand loyalty is so much more fluid than we'd like to think it is. People are purchasing to fill a job that needs to be done. They are shopping the category, not a brand."

Net Promoter Score (NPS) took this a step further. Perhaps someone was going to buy from your brand again out of a lack of imagination or an unwillingness to put thought or effort into the decision. Perhaps it was the only brand that exactly fit their needs, so they felt they had no alternative. Did likelihood to repurchase really mean loyalty? NPS did two radical things. First, it identified brand advocates. Second, it used a simple but very clever way of reframing the data to tell the most compelling story.

Consumers were asked a simple question. How likely are you to recommend this brand to a friend? The correct assumption here is that if you are willing to recommend something, there must be a deeper connection with the brand than just agreement to repurchase. When you recommend something, you put yourself into the narrative. Your opinion is now possibly going to guide someone else's decision. Your recommendation is meaningful. It has weight. It is connected to you. No one wants to have a friend come back to them and say, "*Why did you recommend that? It was awful.*" Advocacy, not repeat purchase, was the true measure of loyalty. If a consumer was willing to put their reputation on the line, there was no greater measure of brand trust and engagement.

Smartly, by shifting the conversation to advocacy, Bain & Company could also start bringing in new metrics that could measure what was happening in the new digital landscape. Online reviews, liking social media posts, posting on social media about the product. These were all new activities and clear ways of measuring advocacy. It was the perfect metric at the perfect time. Companies loved it so much, some actually began tying executive bonuses to the NPS!

The second thing they did was "net" the data. NPS is asked on a 0 to 10 scale. If you gave the brand a 0, you were not at all likely to recommend them to a friend. If you gave the brand a 10, you were extremely likely to recommend them. Typically, researchers would look at the percentage of people who said 9 or 10. That would be considered your highly loyal or strongly advocating target. Just like people can say positive things about your brand, they can also say negative things. While some consumers were becoming co-creators with brands they love, others were more than happy to share their poor experiences with the world and the world was listening.

So, Bain took that percentage of people who said 9 or 10 and subtracted from it those who said 0 through 6. Let's say your brand has 40 percent of people giving you a high NPS rating (9 or 10) and 3 percent giving you a low rating. You would end up with an NPS of 37 percent. That's not a bad story. Now let's say another brand also had 40 percent in their top NPS bucket, but they had a more polarizing experience and had 20 percent in the low bucket. Their NPS score would be 20 percent. By incorporating this "drag" on the number, Bain was able to tell a more nuanced and cautionary story to their clients.

NPS was quickly adopted in the industry. Legacy brand tracking research was retrofitted to include the metric, speakers were showing up at conferences with case studies, and Rebecca and Devora were hearing pressure from clients to incorporate the metric into their own research. One brand that adopted the NPS strategy early was eBay, leveraging the method into what Bain called in 2015 "examples of global best practices" (Markey, 2015). In 2009, the ecommerce marketplace embarked on an effort to implement NPS, eventually crediting it with helping them optimize shipping accuracy, streamline their fees, and implement a buyer protection program. All in the name of loyalty and trust.

The Emergence of Brand Narcissism

While NPS absolutely had advantages and was a smarter way to measure loyalty, Rebecca was still bothered by the idea of measuring loyalty at all. In her experience with qualitative research and talking to shoppers, loyalty wasn't naturally coming up for them. There was the rare superfan, to be sure, but the average consumer was not thinking about the brand first. They were thinking about their own needs first. Rebecca couldn't square the circle. Clients were asking about brand awareness, consideration, and NPS, but it was impossible to find a consumer that thought in those same terms.

In early 2009, right after leaving Hall and Partners, Rebecca had her own lightning bolt moment (in her home office, not a bathtub). Frustrated with a client who wanted the same standard metrics, Rebecca was mulling over how to talk to them about changing what they were asking. "It's just narcissistic," she thought. "The brand wants to know about itself, but the consumer doesn't care about the brand at all." Across from her desk was a framed portrait of one of her favorite monkeys from Cayo Santiago. Letting her brain wander, the lightning bolt struck with a thunderclap. We need to see this from the consumer's point of view, just like researching mating behavior from the female's experience. Brand Narcissism. That was the problem. It would start Rebecca, and then Devora, on a journey to move clients away from this traditional approach to research.

Rebecca often explains Brand Narcissism as like being with a needy date. Imagine being on a date with someone who is wracked with insecurities. All through the dinner, they are peppering you with questions:

"Why did you first decide to go out with me?"
"Have you noticed me on social media?"
"How would you describe me to your friends?"
"What are my personality attributes? Which ones would you like me to have?"
"Would you recommend me as a possible romantic partner to your friends?"
"Will you go out with me again?"

And, the worst one of all:

"How do I compare to the other people you know about?"

Gross, right? You'd quickly find a reason to excuse yourself. But that is exactly what we are asking consumers when we talk to them about brands:

How did you hear about our brand?
Did you see our brand's advertising?
Which of the following best describes our brand?

Select the attributes below that best represent our brand.
Would you recommend our brand to a friend?
Would you be likely to buy this brand again?

Now, repeat all of those questions, but about the competition.

Exhausting. Those may be the questions marketers actually have, fair enough. But that is not the way a consumer thinks when they are making a purchase decision. Think carefully about the last purchase you made. Doesn't matter if it was a coffee or a TV. Did you ever, once, say to yourself, *"Well, I think this brand is trustworthy, but that other brand cares about its customers"* as you were weighing your decision? Never. Not once. Yet all the research out there acts like that is exactly how consumers are thinking about their choices. Our Narcissism Audit helps researchers truly see how their insights might be corrupted by these navel-gazing questions.

This leads us back to the model developed by Starch, enhanced by Howard and then Bain. The purchase funnel. Moving consumers from unaware to aware to familiar to consideration to purchase to advocacy. It worked for a time when the world was simpler—fewer brands, limited distribution, narrow channels for advertising. However, it really bears little reality to the way consumers truly think in today's world.

Hopefully we've convinced you or at least moved you closer to the idea that measuring for loyalty is an outdated practice in research. Now let's look at it from the other end—how the consumer landscape is changing.

KEY TAKEAWAYS

- Revisiting how we ask questions in our research is vital to collecting good insights. We won't find out anything new that drives good business strategy by asking questions in the same way that we always have.

- Brand Narcissism is a barrier to smarter thinking about shoppers. Brands that think like their shoppers do are the ones who stand the best chance of being successful.

- Loyalty is an outdated metric. Companies need to focus on constant acquisition, not take their customers for granted.

References

Bain & Company (2021) Net promoter. www.netpromotersystem.com/about
  (archived at https://perma.cc/7V2E-V7YN)

Christensen, C (2011) *The Innovator's Dilemma: The revolutionary book that will
  change the way you do business*, HarperBusiness, New York

Gladwell, M (2005) *Blink: The power of thinking without thinking*, Little, Brown,
  New York

Howard, J and Sheth, J (1969) *The Theory of Buyer Behavior*, John Wiley & Sons,
  New York

Kahneman, D (2013) *Thinking, Fast and Slow*, Farrar, Straus and Giroux,
  New York

LeCompte, M D (1987) Bias in the biography: Bias and subjectivity in
  ethnographic research, *Anthropology & Education Quarterly*, 18 (1), 43–52

Markey, R (2015) Creating a market of trust and delight at eBay, Bain &
  Company, August 13. www.netpromotersystem.com/insights/creating-a-market-
  of-trust-and-delight-at-ebay-nps-podcast/ (archived at https://perma.cc/
  4HJC-GEJR)

03

The Age of Shopper Promiscuity

In the previous chapter, we laid out flaws in the logic behind measuring consumer loyalty. Applying that focus leads to Brand Narcissism, which ultimately leads brands to act on imperfect information. Like many systems, brand metrics can exist and produce "good enough" results as long as all other things remain relatively stable. However, when the world starts to change sufficiently, the status quo is challenged and those flaws are exposed.

"Let them eat cake," the famous words attributed to (but likely never uttered by) Marie Antoinette prior to the French Revolution, are so often quoted because the phrase is a perfect encapsulation of an out-of-touch ruling class ignoring the clear signs that the status quo was about to change—quite dramatically. In fact, scholars have found versions of this sentence dating back over a hundred years before Marie Antoinette was born.

In order for revolutions to happen, they need two key ingredients: a governing body determined to uphold the current system; and a disillusioned populace willing to take power into its own hands. In our scenario, an adherence to loyalty research is the governing body. This is how we have organized our industry. Lectures have been given, textbooks written, and careers made within this structure. While change in the industry is constantly discussed, those conversations almost invariably center on making tweaks, iterations, and refinements. Like Marie Antoinette, we are not paying attention to our disillusioned populace.

Market research's disillusioned populace—our consumers—isn't crying out for change and demanding anything of us. Rather, our end customers are simply moving on—changing and evolving into a new kind of shopper. We haven't been listening, at least not really. We've been asking about ourselves while shoppers have been taking care of their own needs. And the scary truth is that shopper needs are not reflected in the way most brands and businesses are built to interact with shoppers.

This "revolution" in shopping is really an *evolution* brought on by powerful forces: technology, category disruption, socioeconomics, and more. Shoppers have been given exponentially more choice at a time of significant socioeconomic change. From the global recession of 2008 to the political upheaval on the world stage in the 2010s to the arrival of Covid-19, the world looks very different for shoppers than it did a decade and a half ago. Our research clearly points to a fundamental change—not a shift or an adjustment, but meaningful, lasting change—in the way people shop.

We've coined this evolution as "Shopper Promiscuity." Using the word "promiscuity" is *not* a moral judgment in any way. What we mean by the "promiscuity" part is actually best summed up by Irish poet and playwright Edna O'Brien who said, "Promiscuity is the death of love." In our case, Shopper Promiscuity is the death of loyalty.

We define Shopper Promiscuity as the willingness to try new brands, new products, and new categories. Shopper Promiscuity goes beyond switching brands because of a promotion or coupon. It goes beyond buying a different brand because your preferred brand was out of stock. It even goes beyond having two or three brands in your consideration set. The ways that we've measured "brand switching" in the past are not equipped to reveal the level of Shopper Promiscuity happening now.

Shopper Promiscuity is not a rational decision based on rational inputs. Rather, it is a new state of mind where shoppers *prefer* to explore and try new things. Shoppers are *primed* to want to do that exploring. In many cases, shoppers now prefer to *explore* rather than buy brands they've already experienced. In our latest research conducted in the summer of 2021 exploring recent shoppers, we found that 48 percent of shoppers bought promiscuously. That is, they began their purchase journey with no brand in mind.

Let's stop there for a second and absorb the magnitude of that number. One in two shoppers knew they wanted to purchase in a category, but did not begin their shopping process with a competitive set in mind. Now, put that number in context of the "consideration" question we ask in our surveys. How likely are you to buy this brand in the future? We bet nearly every one of those shoppers would've said they were very likely to buy one or more brands. And yet, nearly one in two of them began shopping completely open to all possibilities.

For brand marketers, that's more than a bit terrifying. We are no longer in the business of building loyalty. We are entering an era of constant acquisition. Every customer must be courted and wooed away from your competitors, even if they have bought from you many times before. We have developed a Shopper Promiscuity Index to help brands understand the extent of the challenge in their category and whether their brand is more or less susceptible to the whims of promiscuous shoppers.

Before we can talk about how to do that, we need to understand what forces are driving this increase in Shopping Promiscuity. For the rest of this chapter, we are going to break out four forces that are putting pressure on shoppers to become more promiscuous: innovation; unlimited access; the need for expression; and reprioritization. Later, in Chapter 8, we will explore what this all means for how research needs to be redefined in this new era.

Driven by Innovation

Consumers understand that advancements in technology are driving innovation at a rapid pace. They live and buy in a world where every year brings a new smartphone or laptop with new and improved features. Look at Apple: they adopted an annual release schedule, promoting a new iPod or iPhone every single year since 2001, with each product always offering *more*. But it's not just tech products where consumers see that dynamic. Now, they can buy robot vacuums controlled by that smartphone or a refrigerator that can tell them, over Wi-Fi, whether there's milk in the house. They can talk to their smart home speaker and ask the machine to play certain music instead of turning the dial on a radio. And even cars—those durable consumer goods—are being stuffed with more and more constantly updating smart tech.

Beyond technology, consumers are also experiencing huge innovations in other categories. Flavor, ingredient, and packaging changes are crowding grocery store shelves with more stock-keeping units (SKUs) than ever before. Strolling down the cookie aisle, you'll see not only dozens of Oreo SKUs in different flavors, but also now in gluten free options. Not to mention the plethora of organics, challenger brands, and other giants elbowing for shelf space. And old experiences are becoming new again: increased access to artisans and tradespeople is bringing "homemade" products to consumers at scale, offering something different than a corporatized product. Further, once stable categories are pushing innovations to basic products. Bedding is a great example: thread count used to be the differentiator that really mattered, but now consumers look for new innovations in materials like incorporating bamboo and/or using sleep science and body thermodynamics to improve the quality of our sleep.

As a result, consumers expect constant change and improvement. They want the latest and the best, and they're open to doing the research to find it. But this isn't just an expectations game. The pace of innovation is increasing so rapidly across every category that it's fundamentally rewiring the shopper brain. The rules have been rewritten such that a changing status quo *is* the status quo. In a world where the customer is always right, shoppers have been programmed to think that they deserve something new, shiny, and leading-edge every single time they buy. And, they're right.

Constant innovation is now table stakes, and that should scare any product or marketing team. If your brand operates in a tech-focused field, you have to continue to think outside the norm and create new experiences, or you'll lose to the competition and you'll do so quickly. If you're in a traditionally stable category, like vacuum cleaners, you still need to understand how consumer expectations are changing and make sure you're delivering new products that are up to date and focused on technological integration. The robot vacuum isn't something from *The Jetsons*. It's here, and the trend of making everything connected and interoperable isn't going to stop: there may be as many as 24.1 billion IoT-connected devices by 2030. The plurality will be consumer devices (Transforma Insights, 2020).

Yet maybe the scariest place to be is in the categories that have long relied on tradition, nostalgia, and limited distribution: consumer packaged goods (CPG). Brands in this space have certainly faced challenges over the last twenty years from newcomers with different ingredient formulations, organics, and more sustainable packaging and sourcing. With the direct-to-consumer explosion of the last five years and the acceleration of online shopping that occurred because of the Covid-19 pandemic, those challenges have grown. However, despite these changes, large brands like Coca-Cola, Nestlé, and Johnson & Johnson have held on to market share. Part of that was through acquisition—Johnson & Johnson alone has acquired 41 other companies (Mergr, 2021). But a significant role was played by dominant brand awareness and consumer familiarity.

Yet, as discussed in the previous chapter, brand awareness is quickly losing relevance. Just because a shopper has heard of a brand does not mean that brand has a significant advantage. In fact, the way shoppers are being retrained to think about the experience flies directly in the face of metrics brands have sought like "A brand I know really well," or "Very familiar with," or "Traditional." Those attributes in general are starting to become more negative than positive. Millennials and Gen Z are not interested in holding on to the past. Gen X has been bored with this conversation since the early 1990s. Boomers are the holdouts, but their buying power will continue to diminish. Any brand banking on their ability to lean into nostalgia and "just like mom used" is destined for the history books.

Driven by Unlimited Access

Over the last decade, in particular, consumers have gotten used to seeing new brands completely disrupt the purchase experience, both for products and services. Direct-to-consumer (DTC) brands like Dollar Shave Club, Hello Fresh, Casper, and Warby Parker have challenged the retail-only paradigm, with the sector's sales estimated at $21 billion in 2021 (eMarketer, 2020). Consumers don't need to rely on a middleman retail company to access the products that they want. DTC isn't just easy and affordable (in most cases), but consumers love the accessibility, customization, and exclusivity that come with buying something straight from the source. "I got this from Target" has a different ring to it than "I got this customized from a cool online brand that's doing things differently." Further, options like subscription boxes and curated product offerings have brought the slick boutique experience to the masses. "Meeting the customer where they are" doesn't just mean figuring out which retailer has a store footprint where you want to be. It means understanding which channels your target customers prefer.

In 2020, YouTube, Instagram, and Pinterest all launched new ecommerce initiatives that will increasingly support in-app purchasing with native payment solutions—allowing shoppers to purchase directly from brands or retailers without leaving the social media platform. This provides powerful opportunities for brands and shoppers to make ads and organic content more "shoppable" as YouTube calls it—but it further complicates life for brands in further expanding on the meaning of multi-channel marketing.

The pace of change isn't just limited to online experiences. Amazon Fresh stores are the online giant's latest attempt to revolutionize in-store grocery shopping. But this isn't about trying to own another shopping channel. Amazon is taking lessons from the success of Amazon Prime and Subscribe and Save to make the experience of in-store shopping much more efficient and pleasant for customers with their "just walk out" system. With this program, Amazon uses technology and AI to determine which products are in your cart. You just leave the store without going through a checkout process (arguably the worst part of the experience for all involved, including the cashiers!) and your account is charged the proper amount later. That kind of program completely upends how we typically think of in-store shopping and might very well catch on if consumers prefer it and Amazon can still make a profit.

The DTC method and Amazon Fresh's brick-and-mortar stores are inventive ways to reimagine a known shopper experience. But tweaking the retail channel by opening an independent web store or leveraging AI to eliminate checkout lines are one thing—inventing a whole new platform to decentralize an entire industry is another. While online marketplaces like eBay, Craigslist, and Etsy allowed consumers to sell products to one another, services weren't wholeheartedly in the mix. Then Uber upended the taxi industry and marked its 10 billionth trip in 2018, just two years after the first billion (Uber, 2018). DoorDash came for restaurant ordering and delivery, now controlling 45 percent of the US food delivery market (Business of Apps, 2021b). AirBnB came for hotels and, despite a global pandemic, notched 193 million reservations in 2020 (Business of Apps, 2021a). These are national online platforms that don't need physical infrastructure like fleets of cars, or a restaurant chain, or a portfolio of boutique hotels. They connect consumers to each other, offering a different experience and posing a threat to entire industry segments. And they did it by innovating in the cloud and putting a free app online.

Ten years ago, people thought nothing of getting in a taxicab with a driver unknown to them. If you had asked us then if we'd feel comfortable getting in someone's personal car who wasn't a licensed taxi driver, we'd have said that it would never happen. Now, Uber or Lyft have completely up-ended that industry. The same is true with AirBnB. The fastest growing hospitality brand does not own any actual property outside of their corporate space.

And consider the restaurant industry. That traditionally very local, low-margin business sector wasn't going to see its hamburgers replaced by an online product—you can't eat smartphone apps. But by giving shoppers an experience that integrates reviews, reservations, coupons, ordering, and delivery, brands like UberEats and DoorDash disrupted how shoppers accessed their food, seizing power from the restaurant and giving it, ostensibly, to the consumer. In the same way we wouldn't have gotten into someone's personal car for a taxi ride, we also wouldn't have dreamed of ordering food without speaking to or visiting the restaurant. But here we are.

Another new favorite disruptor of ours is MrBeast, the YouTube superstar. He opened up a new burger restaurant chain called, inventively, MrBeast Burgers. Seemingly overnight, he had over 300 stores in the US. How? He didn't invest in real estate for stores or build a franchise model or do anything traditional. Partnering with startup Virtual Dining Concepts, MrBeast connected with local mom and pop burger joints and asked if they wanted to sell through the MrBeast Burger app. With a free app to order from, a very streamlined menu, and a fanbase of tens of millions, MrBeast built a profitable national chain restaurant in a matter of months. When surveyed, nearly all of these mom and pop joints that were struggling during the recession marked extremely high sales growth. The shop owners save their businesses. The consumers get a delicious, local interaction with a favorite personality. MrBeast builds an app and collects money. Win, win, win. If McDonald's founder Ray Kroc could see this now!

These new brands caught on so well because the shopping experience they offer has a clear value proposition—a customer-centric experience. And they've had such a massive impact that they forced city, state, and federal governments to consider new public policy. From regulating the gig economy and protecting workers, to limiting the number of AirBnBs allowed in a city, to figuring out how to license and tax Uber and Lyft drivers, governments have faced completely new challenges to a completely new way to do business. While that conversation could be a whole other book, the important takeaway here is that these aren't flash-in-the-pan changes that will fade away. Consumers like them and will continue to seek them out and compare them to traditional offerings.

Industrialists and venture capitalists aren't going to stop with these disruptions either. The money that makes Silicon Valley turn is going to keep chasing the next big disruptor that becomes a unicorn startup company. And that disruptor startup might set out to do one specific thing, then hit on an idea that causes what Larry Downes and Paul Nunes called a "big-bang disruption" in 2015. By offering a different experience that appeals to and is accessible by customers, they can take on entire industries seemingly overnight. With Uber's example, a single customer-to-customer (C2C) services platform idea that threatens a taxi company can travel through the economy and hit your neighborhood restaurant, and then the downtown hotels. What's next?

The brands and shopping channels that emerge in the next ten years are impossible to fully predict. But what we do know is that shoppers are becoming increasingly accustomed to the new and unorthodox. Adoption of these new channels and technologies is happening in real time.

Driven by the Need for Expression

People have always surrounded themselves with symbols. Visual identification and virtue signaling are key components of how we display our affiliations and beliefs. This has also been illustrated in the way people shop. When Rebecca was a child, her father would rail against "Ford" people. Ford, he claimed, was an acronym for *Found On Roadside Dead*. If he saw a Pinto or an Escort, he would delightfully mock the owner as a fool. These kinds of brand identifications have been around for a long time. We understand that what we, and others, buy says something about us. We use purchases to tell our story.

So what's new about today? The primary differentiator is that consumers now face truly expansive choices. Several decades ago, the number of brands consumers could buy was limited by the channels they could physically access. It was easier to choose a brand and its broad associations for yourself because there were just fewer choices to make. Today, the plethora of choice means that every purchase a consumer makes says something more deeply about them. In a world where they could buy so many different things, they bought *that*. And exactly what "that" is carries extra meaning.

When there are so many choices—not just from different brands with "personalities" but also in terms of form, function, environmental impact and sustainability, and political signaling. The reason *why* you chose that brand and product becomes a story. And stories matter. The stories we tell ourselves about who we are, what we believe, and what matters to us are reflected even brighter when every purchase requires thoughtful consideration. Do you buy one jacket because the brand espouses its high environmental standards? Or do you choose a jewelry brand with a solid commitment to human rights? Of course, the jacket and the ring still need to fit in form and price. But consumers also want those items to say something more to their friends and family. Things like "*I'm a good person*" or "*I care about the planet we share.*" It's a deeply personal, intangible thing. But it's real.

There has been a significant shift in the number of companies that are telling their origin stories, seeking to connect consumers directly to the founders and innovators, and building a personal brand identity that customers can adopt as their own. This isn't by accident. Brands are learning that consumers need more than form, function, price, and performance. All other things being equal (or even unequal), consumers want to feel a connection to what they are buying. Compound this internal need for connection with external societal pressure and the need for a story to tell only intensifies. We are going to delve into this more in terms of how shoppers are thinking about the corporations behind brands in Chapter 10, but for now, what matters is that shoppers want their purchases to matter, to have meaning.

Lastly, while we haven't identified this as a force driving Shopper Promiscuity, we would be remiss not to talk about the impact Covid-19 has had on shoppers. Even though technology has been changing our world at such a rapid pace, nothing could have prepared us for the sudden tectonic shift that the pandemic's disruption brought to our daily behavior. It has had such a huge impact that we decided this needed to be explored in much more detail in Chapter 11. Suffice it to say for the purposes of this chapter, Shopper Promiscuity is being encouraged not only by what brands and marketers are doing but also by external forces that are motivating shoppers to quickly change their habits.

Driven by Reprioritization

Value has always been at the forefront of consumer decision making, but recent years have changed what value means in a dramatic way. The first two decades of the 21st century have been a slog for the consumer: terror attacks, multiple military conflicts around the globe, natural disasters, a worsening climate emergency, political turmoil and a global resurgence of authoritarian nationalism, two recessions exacerbating wealth and income inequality, and a global pandemic. It has been exhausting. For most, it hasn't been easy.

We won't attempt to address all of that in this book and we'll leave the details to the experts. However, what we've seen in our research into fear in America is a deep level of distrust and insecurity that can change the way a person operates. Peter Atwater, an economics professor at the College of William and Mary who popularized the idea of a K-shaped recovery, told us how insecurity alters behavior. In times of high insecurity where a majority of people feel vulnerable and at risk, the zeitgeist changes from "us, together, forever" to "me, here, now." Our decisions become laser focused on what is front of us, what will help us get through this, and what matters in the moment (Alter Agents, 2021).

This relates to shopping in a very specific way, because dollars are the resources we have to protect ourselves in uncertain moments—we use them to buy emotional or physical security. So when consumers feel pessimistic or scared, every dollar spent has to mean something. The trade-offs of what else you could spend your money on and the stakes of not spending it on meaningful relief are higher. Especially when financial burden is added to the mix, that means taking economic tradeoffs. Many parents during the Covid-19 pandemic were forced to decide between continuing to work or staying home to manage childcare, for instance. But these tradeoffs can come in many different forms (MFour, 2021).

Sometimes, money is spent with the aim of reducing stress, increasing convenience or even just giving a moment's jolt of serotonin—we saw plenty of that during the pandemic. The future risk of financial instability gets overshadowed by the need for self-care at the moment. Longer-term goals and plans might be postponed as we focus on "me, here, now" just to get by. All of this points to different influences and increased stress in shopping decisions. Like after the Great Depression, we have seen a major shift in how people think about their safety in the world, social justice, corporate responsibility, and "needs" vs "wants." And it makes them reprioritize their resources.

At the beginning of the millennium, no one could have predicted the impact that smartphones would have on the world. Who knows what new developments are on the horizon that will once again rewire our behavior? Change is the status quo, which means consumers are forever open to new brands. And loyalty, as we've defined it, is irrelevant.

What does this all mean? In short, nothing in the future will look like the past or even like our present. Tweaking the model, iterating on past experiences, making adjustments—none of that will be enough for a brand to survive and thrive in the future. The power has been shifting slowly to the customer for the last two decades, but that shift is rapidly accelerating and there will not be a pendulum swing back to the days when brands held all the cards. We have trained shoppers to expect the best, to assume that the best is actually table stakes, and we have given them unlimited choice. The consumer is unbound and powerful. In turn, research must also avoid the lure of tweaking models and stepping stone iterations. Just like how MrBeast,

Uber, and AirBnB disrupted old systems, the research industry is calling out for a completely new approach.

Over these last two chapters, we have shared a lot of theory. Ideas about Brand Narcissism, Promiscuous Shopping, and the forces that will irrevocably reshape our future. Theory is the starting point. As researchers, we have to prove out these hypotheses with data.

In 2021, our company conducted our own research on Shopper Promiscuity. With a sample of 6,000 recent purchasers, we explored shopping behaviors in six different categories to reveal how shoppers are making decisions. This research was designed from the shopper's perspective. What needs were they trying to meet? What actions did they take? How influential were those actions on their final purchase decision? What barriers did they face during the process? Note, none of these are from the brand's point of view (*"Have you heard of me?" "Do you like me?"*). Yet, we believe absolutely that the results from these questions ultimately will prove illuminating and actionable. Let's get to the data.

KEY TAKEAWAYS

- Technology, social upheaval, and economic disruption have fueled the rise of Shopper Promiscuity. Customers aren't acquired for life—they're won or lost at every single purchase decision.

- Seemingly unlimited access and constant innovation push shoppers to always look for something better. Companies that want to stay ahead of the game need to actively monitor for disruptors and do some disrupting to their own businesses too.

- Shoppers use their purchases as a means of self-expression. What they buy says something about their identities and priorities.

References

Alter Agents (2021) *Facing Fear: Overcoming consumer anxiety.* https://alteragents.com/wp-content/uploads/2021/01/Facing-Fear-III-full-res.pdf (archived at https://perma.cc/ZSP3-G9F7)

Business of Apps (2021a) Airbnb revenue and usage statistics, Business of Apps. www.businessofapps.com/data/airbnb-statistics/ (archived at https://perma.cc/A5LT-X6KV)

Business of Apps (2021b) DoorDash revenue and usage statistics, Business of Apps. www.businessofapps.com/data/doordash-statistics/ (archived at https://perma.cc/WG47-A3G9)

Downes, L and Nunes, P (2015) Big-bang disruption, *Harvard Business Review*, March. hbr.org/2013/03/big-bang-disruption (archived at https://perma.cc/84FG-2YL6)

eMarketer (2020) US direct-to-consumer ecommerce sales will rise to nearly $18 billion in 2020, eMarketer, April 2. www.emarketer.com/newsroom/index.php/us-direct-to-consumer-ecommerce-sales-will-rise-to-nearly-18-billion-in-2020/ (archived at https://perma.cc/6836-RGA5)

Mergr (2021) Johnson & Johnson mergers and acquisitions summary, Mergr. https://mergr.com/johnson-%26-johnson-acquisitions#:%7E:text=Johnson%20%26%20Johnson%20has%20acquired%2041,came%20from%20private%20equity%20firms (archived at https://perma.cc/AVV7-WG8L)

MFour (2021) Here's why 49% buy luxury products in a pandemic. https://mfour.com/blog/under-pressure-49-buy-luxury-products-in-pandemic/ (archived at https://perma.cc/CT6G-6WWP)

Transforma Insights (2020) Global IoT market will grow to 24.1 billion devices in 2030, generating $1.5 trillion annual revenue. www.prnewswire.com/news-releases/global-iot-market-will-grow-to-24-1-billion-devices-in-2030--generating-1-5-trillion-annual-revenue-301061873.html (archived at https://perma.cc/W55P-ARMN)

Uber (2018) 10 billion, Uber, July 24. www.uber.com/newsroom/10-billion/ (archived at https://perma.cc/4F9X-93XF)

04

The Shopper DIAL

We discussed how brand loyalty became the hero of marketing and advertising research over the past hundred years or so. Additionally, we examined the forces of change that are pushing consumers to be more promiscuous in shopping behaviors and purchase decisions. Here comes the hard part: what do we do about all of that? It's one thing to point out an issue, but it's another to solve it.

For these next few chapters, we are going to be diving deep into our research methodology and findings. Over the last decade, we have been doing shopper research for brands, retailers, and agencies which has revealed the rise of Shopper Promiscuity and the challenges these brands face in this new environment. In addition to our client work, in 2021 we surveyed 6,000 Americans on recent purchases they made using our proprietary Shopper Promiscuity metrics. The data referenced now will be full of insights about Shopper Promiscuity patterns in total, by different categories, and by demographics. More importantly, there is not a single bit of Brand Narcissism in this research. Rather, everything is considered from the shopper's perspective, priorities, and needs. We are very excited to be able to finally share the revolutionary work we've been discussing with clients for the last ten years.

The Correct Research Audience?

First, let's start with the research respondent. This is the person who answers our questions—whether online, on the phone, or in person. Too often in our industry, people are often conflated into one broad group: consumers. While we are all consumers, yes, there is a critical dynamic that moves us from inactive to active states. Our research has demonstrated time and again that who you talk to and how active they are in the category are critically important. Unfortunately, many in our industry are talking to the wrong people.

We break down respondents into three broad groups:

- **Non-intenders:** People who are not intending to buy in the category.
- **Intenders:** People who intend to buy within a certain time frame.
- **Purchasers:** People who have purchased in the category.

Talking to Non-intenders is relatively pointless when you're trying to understand how to market your brand to interested consumers. Talking to Purchasers has traditionally been thought of as a "rear view" approach that fails to capture the messages and triggers that could influence the decisions before purchase. We had initially fallen into that same way of thinking, but came to realize that *Recent* Purchasers were actually the best, and really the only valid group to research. We'll take you through how our company came to that decision later, but let's start with where the industry focuses—Intenders.

Intenders seem, on the surface, to be exactly the group researchers want to speak with. They are interested in the category. They are active in the shopping process and can speak clearly to their opinions of the brands they are encountering. When we were first beginning our shopper research at Alter Agents, Intenders seemed like the perfect group. We could ask them about their journey, what they were doing, what they had done, what was left to do. We could talk to them about the brands they are considering and why those brands were on their mind. Plus, they would be actively doing exactly what we are researching—shopping.

Surprisingly, our projects that revealed Intenders' answers about what they would do and, ultimately, what they would purchase, were not resulting in new insights. The problem is that everything these respondents will answer is speculative and generic. Big brands always win in these surveys because respondents are not critically thinking about their opinions. *Is Whirlpool a trustworthy brand?* A respondent who is intending to purchase would likely answer "Yes." They answer yes because Whirlpool is a known brand, because they assume a brand that big will be trustworthy, but most importantly because they haven't had to place their money on an opinion yet. They are making assumptions and estimates about future behavior.

Numerous studies have been conducted in the fields of psychology, sociology, and anthropology that highlight the gaps between what we say we are going to do and what we actually do. Survey respondents also often represent their "best selves" in their survey responses. Noted archaeologist and founder of the sub-field "garbology" William Rathje famously asked Americans what they had in their home. Then, a week later, he went through their garbage (with their permission, of course). What he found should not be surprising. People surveyed dramatically underrepresented the amount of alcohol and tobacco they were consuming. In addition, the number of processed foods they said they were eating was far lower than the amounts indicated by the packaging they had discarded (Rathje and Murphy, 2001).

There are several reasons people do this—they feel a need to represent themselves in the best light, experience self-delusion about their own "bad habits," or need to minimize the negative things in their lives. Regardless of the reasons why, it was clear that there was a disconnect between what people said they did and what they actually did. But even if you had the most objective, unbiased respondent, the intention still wouldn't be a strong predictor of their ultimate decision. Intention offers a decent chance of what might happen, but no shopper can predict their mood in the moment, their exposure to persuasive advertising, or whether promotions might pop up to sway their thinking. Yet, despite clear evidence that "intention" is poorly correlated with "action," it is still a common approach in research.

Then why doesn't our industry talk to people who purchased? Recent Purchasers can give you more accurate information having just completed their journey. They will remember what they researched and how, what brand they bought and why, and what their concerns or hesitations were. True, no self-reported survey is 100 percent free of the errors of human memory, but Recent Purchasers at least have clarity on what they did and why they did it. But the reason this group is often ignored has much more to do with logistics than insights. Recent Purchasers are a much smaller subset of the population. Finding people to take surveys, participate in focus groups, and answer phone calls from strangers is exhausting work. The harder it is to find who you want to talk to, the more expensive finding and incentivizing that person becomes. Ultimately, our industry is a business ruled by budgets as well as best practices and we have come to see Intenders as "good enough" for the information we need.

When our shopper journey research began in 2010, we were of the same mind. We believed that Intenders were good enough and we were used to interpreting data from this group. However, as data started coming in, we noticed that there was little variation in the data. People seemed to be shopping in different categories quite similarly. There was also not a lot of differentiation among shoppers within the same category. The amount of homogeneity we saw in the data was an indicator that we were not getting the full picture. They were not, in fact, good enough.

We had a theory that the data looked this way because the questions themselves were wrong. Rebecca was trained to think like an anthropologist. How is her experience and perspective influencing the observations she's making? Devora was trained to think like a retailer and marketer. She recognized the data lacked the kind of power and insight to excite marketers. Together, they wondered if the people themselves were the wrong subjects to study. Why ask people what they think they will do when we can simply ask people what they did.

After a few studies comparing Intenders to Purchasers, it was abundantly clear that Intenders' views and opinions were too broad to be helpful at best and misleading at worst. Recent Purchaser insights, however, yielded meaningful differentiation between categories. Suddenly, shopping for home improvement products did look different than shopping for a car. More importantly, there was variation within the category. New groups of spontaneous shoppers emerged, or those who were heavily influenced by social media and nothing else. Recent Purchasers were revealing completely new behaviors and attitudes that were marked or even unknown when Intenders were left to hypothesize.

While we were very excited about the data, it was more of a challenge to get our clients excited about the increase in their budgets. So, for a time, we had to ask for an augment of Recent Purchasers alongside Intenders. We stood our ground that the Recent Purchasers would provide critical insights, so most clients begrudgingly funded a small sub-sample of Recent Purchasers. In every single instance, once they saw the data coming back from these two groups, the Intenders were quickly set aside and the conversation centered on the information coming from Recent Purchasers. After we developed a few case studies, it became very clear to our new clients that Recent Purchasers were worth the extra budget.

Defining Shopper Promiscuity

Now that we've identified who we need to talk to, let's define Shopper Promiscuity and how we measure it. Shopper Promiscuity is a complicated metric and cannot be reduced to a simple "likelihood" scale. When exploring ways to measure Shopper Promiscuity, we kept the following three primary questions in mind:

- **Shopper Impulsivity:** How long does it take for shoppers to go from undecided to decided?

- **Brand Ambivalence:** Where does the brand come into play in the shopper journey?

- **Brand Loyalty:** If they start with a brand in mind, how likely are they to actually purchase that brand?

Why these questions? Let's take them each in turn.

Shopper Impulsivity

Shopper Impulsivity measures how quickly people make their decisions. In every category, there is a range from a deep researcher who ponders their options over a long period, to the shopper that decides immediately in the moment. Most marketers and researchers think of this in terms of "high and low consideration" categories. For example, automotive purchases are often represented as a "high consideration" category. There is an assumption that laying out that much of a financial commitment would motivate a customer to take time reviewing their options, talk with friends and family, and have a couple of test drives. The perception is that there is a long lead time from deciding to buy a car to making a purchase. A "low consideration" category might be pancake mix, where shoppers default to known brands and take very little time (if any at all) to research their choice before buying.

To a certain extent, these broad categorizations are true. But in every one of the several dozens of categories we have done this research for, there is always a surprisingly large minority of shoppers who buck these assumptions. In automotive, for example, we have consistently seen about 10–15 percent of shoppers making their decisions in 48 hours or less. Now, you might be thinking of a stereotypical rich person who can be cavalier about those decisions, but it crosses demographics. A car breaking down or being totaled, a surprise gift for a college grad, an amazing deal that brought a new-to-the-category shopper to the dealer's lot combined with a persuasive salesman—any one of these and countless other reasons can lead to rapid decision making in this "high consideration" category. To be entirely candid, Rebecca cannot tolerate decisions that take a long time to make and has bought several cars after walking onto a lot that same day. These shoppers exist, and their shopping styles are largely being ignored by the research industry.

But it isn't only a spontaneous mindset. Many times, the situation itself can lead to more spontaneous behavior. A favorite example of ours is to think about two women who want to purchase new dishwashers. One is remodeling her kitchen and wants the perfect appliance that not only functions exactly as she wants, but looks perfect with the remodel. The other shopper had a dishwasher break down two days before her family was coming for Thanksgiving. She needs something in stock that can be delivered and installed before a holiday. Their shopper journeys are going to be wildly different. Still, both are valid and both present excellent opportunities for brands to win those customers.

The same is true in "low consideration" categories. We brought up pancake mix because it has quickly become a very complicated category. There are now protein-infused, gluten-free, whole grain, and many other options out there each touting unique benefits to the consumer. The pancake mix decision has become complicated. In our research, we have seen a meaningful minority of consumers who take quite some time to go from indecision to decision. Suppose a shopper was recently diagnosed with a health condition that requires them to rethink the things they buy. Perhaps a home chef is sourcing the best ingredients for their newest kitchen creation. To paint this category with the "low consideration" brush washes out all of the variations in shopping styles.

It is this variation where the interesting details lie and where we have found many insights that have brought our clients new and meaningful ways to alter their businesses. Our research captures a very specific and detailed timeline of the shopping process. We incorporate a timeline ranging from a few moments before purchase to months or more depending on the category. Individual respondent answers are then mapped to their research and behaviors during the shopping process.

Loyalty has an interesting interplay with impulsivity. Some impulse purchases are simply replacing beloved products. The shopper sees a favorite brand and buys. Simple. But impulsive purchases can also be about trying something new—a new brand, a new feature, or a new color. Understanding the interplay between loyalty and impulsivity is essential.

Brand Ambivalence

Brand Ambivalence is the next layer of Shopper Promiscuity, involving how likely a brand is to come into play at the beginning of the shopper's journey. As we will show you later in this chapter, on average, half of consumers begin their shopping journey without a specific brand in mind. Let's pause on that for a moment, because that is a very large number. Think of all the advertising dollars that are spent on building brand awareness and consideration. Why, given the billions of dollars spent per year in the US alone on brand-building advertising, do nearly one in two shoppers go into a category without any brand in mind? It could be that those dollars are not convincing people or being seen. However, we know people are seeing advertising, and in most cases it is benign if not enjoyable content. We don't think advertising content and reach is the problem.

The alternative is that those shoppers have seen the ads, maybe even enjoyed watching the ads, or have a jingle stuck in their head, but the brand is not driving the shopper's journey. The brand is not the hero accompanying the shopper through this process and giving shoppers the confidence they need to settle on the right product—their brand's product. Marketers and advertisers have assumed they have a role in shoppers' minds. An important role. But the reality is for every shopper, including you, dear reader, we are the heroes of our own shopping stories. We are the ones experiencing the narrative and the brand is, at best, allowed to tag along or, more likely, irrelevant.

Ambivalence can vary widely by category. One of the most fascinating categories we've researched on this issue is soft drinks. Out of the dozens of categories we've studied, it was the only one with ambivalence scores that fell below 40 percent of shoppers. In fact, it wasn't just lower than the others, it cratered to the bottom at a measly four percent of shoppers. Only four percent of shoppers started their soft drink purchase journey without a brand in mind. If shoppers want a soft drink, they nearly universally already know what they are going to buy before the transaction is made. Is this category Shopper Promiscuity-proof? Not exactly. While loyalty is still quite high among soft drink consumers, the pool of soft drink consumers is shrinking rapidly every year. The Shopper Promiscuity here is not between different soft drink brands but between soft drinks and alternative beverages.

Ambivalence is rarely addressed in research. We start with the concept of a consideration set: what brand or brands are shoppers considering at the outset? When we ask Intenders this question, they can easily answer with brands that come top of mind or brands they've used before. This reinforces our marketing decisions—we have high brand awareness! But as pointed out above, these are hypotheticals. When asked, Rebecca could easily recall three or four kitchen appliance brands and would answer that it was likely she would purchase one of those. However, when she starts her journey, she is thinking about what she really needs: a new toaster oven that can handle the volume of chicken nuggets her children are consuming. She's not thinking about the differences in brand personality between Breville and General Electric. Her needs are the most important. She's the chicken nugget hero here.

Our research found that about half of shoppers begin their journey ambivalent about brands. How does that number square with the research you have seen on your own brand? Because our industry tends to feed clients' Brand Narcissism, it is likely a surprise to think of any category being that vulnerable to Shopper Promiscuity. But that is exactly what Brand Narcissism does. It reframes the shopper's actual experience to fit the preconceptions of the brand. It does not reflect reality.

Brand Loyalty

Brand Loyalty encompasses the other roughly half of the population that does start with a brand in mind. Maybe they need to restock their favorite toothpaste or they have a strong preference for a makeup brand. These are the folks that marketers and advertisers have been thinking of and targeting. But they are only half the population… for now. Rather than rely on hypothetical decisions from shoppers, our metric is quite simple. Did they buy the brand they had in mind at the start of the purchase journey? Rooted in fact, it provides a much clearer picture of the role brand plays in the shopper's experience.

Shopper Impulsivity, Brand Ambivalence, and Brand Loyalty are the pillars of our Shopper Promiscuity research. By understanding how people shop the category, the role brands play and when the brand enters the journey, we can map out a story based on reality, not conjecture, that marketers and advertisers can actually use to move the dial.

The Facets of Shopper Promiscuity

Using the framework of our three Shopper Promiscuity pillars, we have developed a categorization system of respondents called the Shopper DIAL. The DIAL stands for our four types of shoppers:

- **Defectors:** Shoppers who started with a brand in mind, but bought a different brand.

- **Impulsives:** Shoppers who bought spontaneously in the moment.

- **Ambivalents:** Shoppers who did not have a brand in mind when they started shopping.

- **Loyalists:** Shoppers who began with a brand in mind and purchased that brand.

Stepping out of acronym order for a minute, let's talk about the *Impulsives*. Impulsives might or might not have a brand in mind when they decided to purchase. It is a matter of moments, seconds, even, from the spontaneous decision that you want something to purchasing the item. What makes Impulsives interesting as a group is that they have a very limited time in which they can be influenced by information. In those few moments, they can take several actions—search online for better prices, look up customer reviews, text a photo of the product to a friend, etc. It is unfair to say that Impulsives do no research. We've found the opposite. In our research, Impulsives use nearly as many sources of information to make their decision before purchasing as shoppers that take days or more.

This means that Impulsives are open to persuasion and information that might sway their decision, no matter how brief the moment of indecision is. Spontaneity does not mean that these shoppers should be disregarded. To that end, after identifying the number of Impulsives we have in the study, we then group them with the rest of the DIAL based on where the brand came into play for them. What we have found intriguing and what has helped our clients make smarter marketing decisions, is the extent to which shopping in their category is impulsive. Is it like automotive with a small, but meaningful number? Is it like the snack food category which is dominated by Impulsives? Even more importantly, how does their brand rate against the category average? Are shoppers more likely to shop spontaneously when buying their product, and be more considered when buying from their competitors?

We categorize shoppers into the remaining three DIAL groups based on where the brand entered the shopper journey. For *Loyalists* and *Defectors*, the brand was at the beginning of the journey. They had a specific brand in mind from the start. Loyalists purchased that brand and, for some reason, Defectors did not. Overall, on average these two groups combined make up about half of shoppers. No matter what category we research, Defectors are always a small minority, usually under 5 percent of shoppers. This tells us something really interesting. If a brand is present at the beginning of the journey, it takes a great deal to sway shoppers away from that brand. This is the loyalty that marketers are seeking. But it is striking that, regardless of the category, typically only half of shoppers begin with a brand in mind.

DIAL Demographics

At this point, you might be thinking this is great news. Half of shoppers are brand loyal and they almost always buy the brand they had in mind. So, what is the point of this book? Well, there is one very stark piece of data that encapsulates the entire reason why we have to acknowledge and explore Shopper Promiscuity. The proportion of loyal shoppers decreases dramatically by generation.

FIGURE 4.1   Share of shoppers in each generation who bought a product from the same brand they were considering at the start of the shopping journey

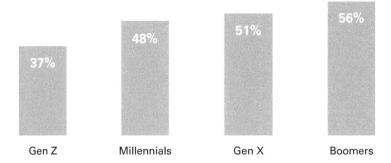

There is a 19 percentage point gap between Boomers and Gen Z in terms of Loyalist shoppers. Many of the forces that impact and drive Shopper Promiscuity that we discussed in the last chapter are not changes for Gen Z, but represent the way the world has always been for them. Gen Z are digital natives. They grew up with cable internet; no dial-up screeching in their lives. They had their own smartphones in middle school and high school. Online shopping has always been an option for them. This group did not have to adjust to a new reality like the generations before them. This has always been their normal and it will continue to be this way for the generations to come. Digital accessibility has changed our future shoppers permanently.

Gen X and Millennials could be considered transitional generations. Their shopping habits and attitudes were formed at a time before the internet or while it was still in its infancy. However, their lower loyalty levels overall point to an ability to adapt and change to the new normal. We are at an inflection point in the history of shopping. The generations that come after Gen Z will continue this trend as they become the second generation of digital natives growing up in homes run by their Millennial parents.

When the household is out of something she wants, Rebecca's seven-year-old daughter rolls her eyes and asks Alexa to put it on the shopping list. How do you explain to this child what the world used to be like twenty years ago? Of course she and millions of future shoppers like her are going to expect innovation, connection, and quality at their fingertips. We have trained them for this. This decline in loyalty is a trend our shopper research has been showing for more than a decade. The brands that succeed in the future are those that are reorienting towards the promiscuous shopper now.

Age is not the only interesting demographic trend we see in Shopper Promiscuity. Income also plays a major role. Loyalty, it turns out, is more of a privilege for wealthier consumers. Households with above-average incomes are more likely to be loyal to a brand and less likely to shop impulsively. Households with below-average income are significantly more likely to defect from an intended brand, be ambivalent when entering the category, and to shop impulsively. Let's start with Defectors. Some of the reasons why people would move from their intended brand are rational—the item was out of stock, or another brand had a better price. Price is an easier barrier for wealthier shoppers to overcome, reducing the likelihood that they'll defect.

But wealthier consumers are also less likely to be ambivalent, meaning they more often start with a brand in mind. Perhaps a more stable income gives wealthier consumers the luxury of being able to think about brands more as opposed to having to buy what can be afforded at the moment. Our research shows that a family that has just remodeled their kitchen would have a much different shopping journey when buying new appliances than a low-income family whose necessary equipment just broke down. The former has the time and finances to consider brands. The latter simply needs something that will work right now.

In our work with Peter Atwater, an economist and professor at the College of William and Mary, we discussed the K-shaped recovery following the Covid-19 recession. This economic model shows a very positive recovery for some (the upper arm of the K) while other segments of the population (the lower leg of the K) experience stagnation or a continued economic decline. With the post-Covid economy, the trend towards more automation in service work, and economic barriers to education, we are likely to see a widening gap in our economy between the haves and have nots. Below-average-income households are the current majority of homes in the US and will not be diminishing in size any time soon. Most brands serve these folks and they have needs that are driving them away from brand affinity.

FIGURE 4.2   Share of each household income bracket sorted into the Loyalist, Defector, Ambivalent, and Impulsive shopper categories

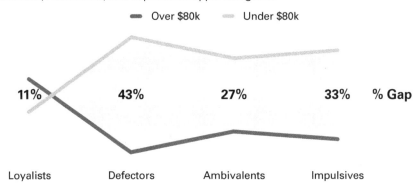

Women also exhibit significantly higher levels of Shopper Promiscuity. It's a trend that holds regardless of the generation these women are in. Women are typically responsible for the bulk of purchases in the household. A recent widely-cited report from Bloomberg found that women were driving 70–80 percent of all consumer purchase decisions, either through buying power or influence (Nelson, 2020). In turn, that means the bulk of purchase decisions are made by promiscuous shoppers.

Why would women trend towards more promiscuous shopping behavior than men? Certainly, the forces driving Shopper Promiscuity are impacting both genders. Yet, women are more likely to start their purchase journey without a brand in mind. Additionally, those who do start with a brand in mind are significantly more likely to defect to a different brand than men. The truth lies in many different factors that impact the way men and women approach shopping. In particular, that women continue to earn less than men, forcing them into more difficult economic choices that can lead to promiscuous shopping behavior. Nothing in our data reveals a clear reason for the gender gap, but brands that cater to women or women's influence need to be even more vigilant about the impact of Shopper Promiscuity.

FIGURE 4.3   Share of each principal gender sorted into the Loyalist, Defector, Ambivalent, and Impulsive shopper categories

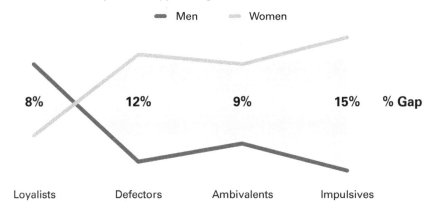

Stepping back to look broadly at these trends, we see that older, higher-income, or males are the most likely groups to be loyal. Older, higher-income males have been the architects of the fields of marketing, product development, and market research for the last hundred years. This adherence to loyalty we discussed in the previous chapter more accurately reflects the shopping experience of those developing the models than the actual shoppers. Market research built a system of shopper understanding based on our own reflection.

Anthropologists, ethnographers, journalists, and any other profession that attempts to understand human behavior are all aware that everything they see is filtered through a personal lens forged by their own experiences, backgrounds, and socioeconomic status. Trial lawyers could spend hours, maybe days, discussing how multiple witnesses can see the same event but interpret that event in entirely different ways. The same must hold for those of us who research human behavior in the market research profession. We see ourselves reflected back and minimize or ignore the stories that do not fit the narrative we understand. The decline of loyalty among younger shoppers makes it evident that we can no longer analyze our own reflections, but must see the world through the lens of the shopper.

What the Shopper DIAL Tells Us

How do we prevent ourselves from viewing the world through our eyes? By asking the right questions. Brand Narcissism exists because we want consumers to tell us what they think of our brands. We genuinely want to improve our products, solve their problems, and serve our consumers. But the questions are all wrong. Our solution to this dilemma is to reframe the entire experience through the shopper's lens and ask them why they made those choices.

In our decade of researching this DIAL, our clients are consistently learning new insights that reshape their business. Traditional research tells brands if people like them, who likes them, and what those people think about their competitors. It does not focus on actual behavior and it does not see the world from the shopper's point of view. This has led to myopia, focusing only on brand, talking about brand, and trying to improve the brand connection. But brand is only one component, and in some cases a miniscule component, of the decision's factors. Yes, brand love is great when it happens, but we need to count on that happening less and less over time. If a brand is focused on creating brand love, what opportunities are they missing to gain real market share and influence shoppers?

The Shopper DIAL answers several key questions for brands:

- **Defectors** represent the opportunity to sway intention into a new action. Why did people defect? What opportunities are there for your brand to intercept potential Defectors? There are two sides to this coin. Understanding the shoppers that defected *from* your brand (they had intended to buy yours, but didn't) to those that defected *to* your brand (they intended to buy another brand and bought yours instead). Learning how your brand attracted and repelled customers is critical in today's promiscuous shopping environment. Every customer, whether they've bought your brand before or not, needs to be re-acquired. Knowing what persuaded them from, or to, a brand is a powerful insight.

- **Impulsives** are making rapid decisions but still research and explore before buying. What information does your brand offer that is easy to find and digest? How are you providing confidence to shoppers that they are making the right choice? One of the key issues that brands consistently get wrong is underestimating how much information consumers want. We are constantly told that attention spans are slipping and people don't want to wallow in the details. However, our research has shown that shoppers are hungry for information. Brands that deliver information in a variety of different ways and through different channels will succeed.

- **Ambivalents** begin the shopping process without a brand in mind. What is their journey towards purchase? When and how does the brand get introduced to these shoppers? At some point shoppers have to purchase an actual brand. But how many shoppers can name the brand they purchased? Depending on the category, it actually can be quite different. We've done a lot of work in the home improvement space, for example, and find that brand recognition even among Recent Purchasers can be quite low. This would imply then that brand is not a meaningful factor in their decision making. Exploring Ambivalents gives us clear insight into where they intersect with the brand in the shopper journey and how influential it is.

- **Loyalists** bought their intended brand. Where does your brand sit in comparison to the category average? Do you over- or under-index on Loyalists? How are you reinforcing your brand for these shoppers? While this group is in decline, they are still here and can have many important lessons to teach us. Loyalists, in our view, are not synonymous with high Net Promoter Scores or strong consideration numbers. These are people who actually acted on that brand love. Revealing this prized group can help our clients cling to them and attempt to replicate them for as long as possible.

Establishing the DIAL and share of promiscuous shopping being done in a category is only the beginning. The next piece of the puzzle is understanding what these consumers do as they move from undecided to decided. What information are they actively looking for? Where are they going for that information? How influential is it? The DIAL reveals promiscuous shopping segments, but it does not take us through the journey with the shopper.

In the next few chapters, we will answer all of those questions and demonstrate how much more meaningful this data can be for marketers and advertisers instead of familiarity, consideration, and brand engagement metrics.

KEY TAKEAWAYS

- The most actionable data doesn't come from purchase Intenders. It comes from actual Recent Purchasers who can tell you exactly what they did and why they did it.

- Shopper Promiscuity and brand ambivalence vary widely across categories and demographics. Brands need to understand the evolving preferences that affect their category and vertical.

- The DIAL—Defectors, Impulsives, Ambivalents, and Loyalists—is a useful framework for understanding the shoppers in your market.

References

Nelson, A (2020) Women drive majority of consumer purchasing and it's time to meet their needs, Inc.com, July 17. www.inc.com/amy-nelson/women-drive-majority-of-consumer-purchasing-its-time-to-meet-their-needs.html (archived at https://perma.cc/YE8M-KL2N)

Rathje, W and Murphy, C (2001) *Rubbish! The archaeology of garbage*, University of Arizona Press, Tucson

05

Source Usage

A New Metric for Changing Shopper Behavior

One of the foundations—the gravy train you could say—of the research industry is brand and ad tracking research. We talked in a prior chapter about narcissistic brand research as focused on questions that sound like they come from a needy date. *Did you notice me? Do you remember when you first saw me? How do I compare to everyone else?* Philosophically, we have serious objections to the premise behind research like that. But there's another problem. Traditional ad tracking research isn't just narcissistic. It's also incredibly narrow and remarkably difficult to act upon.

Brand and ad tracking research shows respondents ads that are currently running across media. They are presented with screenshots or snippets of TV ads, print ads, and maybe even radio content or outdoor billboards. The questioning follows a three-step process. First, *Have you seen this?* Second, *Who is the sponsor of the ad?* And third, there's a question focusing on some form of engagement metric to measure efficacy, such as, *Did this increase your interest in buying brand X?* As discussed in the last chapter, it is industry standard to ask these questions of Intenders in the category.

Because brand and ad tracking research is all about what respondents have already seen, it only observes awareness. This is problematic because it doesn't explain how effective or useful that advertising was to the shopper—only whether your marketing team is meeting their current ad investment key performance indicators (KPIs) or not. What it doesn't do is open up the universe beyond what you already know or reveal where else shoppers are being influenced, likely by your competitors.

The difference between that approach and ours is that our research shows what was actually used in making decisions, not what was seen. We'll talk later about our Net Influence metric, which reveals whether a touchpoint has actually influenced a purchase decision, but first let's start with our first critical metric, Source Usage.

Why Source Usage Matters

Source Usage reveals what sources or touchpoints shoppers use along their path to purchase. And, it is also the metric that changed our entire perspective on the shopper journey. We didn't actually realize when we first designed Source Usage how useful it would be—we were just trying to figure out a new way to understand what was actually making a difference to shoppers in their purchase decisions. Over time, we began to see that this metric we'd had the spark to create was a powerful proxy for consideration. But, more than that, it reveals how much shoppers care about the category in which they are buying. As it turns out, it is also one of the best indicators of the increasing Shopper Promiscuity that we covered in the prior chapter.

Simply put, the more sources a shopper uses, the more research they are doing prior to purchase. The more research they are doing, the more invested they are in their decision. Invested doesn't mean that they are thrilled with their purchase—we'll get to Source Usage as entertainment in a moment. But them being invested means that there are reasons driving the shopper to spend more time and effort doing more research than we might otherwise expect. Those reasons could come from so many different places. It could be that they are the type of shopper who just feels the need to know everything. Or perhaps they don't yet understand the category in which they are buying in because, like a new mom buying a crib for the first time or a Gen Zer buying their first car, they haven't had to before. Their investment might be driven by their values, like sustainability or human rights. It could be because they view the purchase as risky, or because the category itself is complicated and has a lot of different issues to consider. Or, in some cases, it's because people just really like researching products in that category and the research itself becomes part of the enjoyment of the product and an entertainment experience. Regardless of the reasons that drive a shopper's investment in the process, we know that they're doing more of it and that those reasons tell us an important story.

More than anything else, it's the dynamic of the product category that determines the type and number of sources a shopper uses. It's also important to note that some shopper archetypes consistently do more research and are more anxious ahead of purchasing than others. And some do hardly any research. However, for any given category there are always things that drive some shoppers who are not typically researchers to kick into high gear—and there are some shoppers who typically research everything and then find themselves one day buying a car sight unseen. That's what makes this work so fascinating. Source Usage is, for us, a view of what shoppers value and what they are willing to risk. What could be more exciting than a metric that tells us that?!

Now you understand why we still talk about Source Usage like it's the first time we've ever discovered it—because literally, for every category we study, Source Usage is different and changing over time. You can begin to see how powerful this can be for brands. Suddenly, there's a single number that helps reveal shoppers' level of passion, engagement, and interest in a particular category. Where it gets really fun is being able to compare this number at the brand level—and, literally, all the competitive brand marketing efforts become laid bare. You can see where your competition is investing in social media or influencer marketing, or where another brand is playing heavily in online videos, or how another clearly has their retail sales strategy down pat. It's powerful stuff that can drive some truly informed business decisions.

Several years ago, we did work for a leading premium headphones brand—in fact, their product was the best on the market, and it wasn't even close. We saw immediately in the Source Usage findings that the category saw intense levels of research, even for shoppers who were making their decision in a relatively short period of time. But when we drilled down to the brand level, there was clearly one competitor of our client's that had off-the-chart levels of Source Usage. The shoppers buying that brand were using many more sources on average compared to the other brands we researched. And not only that, shoppers buying from this competitor brand—which has since witnessed exponential growth—were using different sources than shoppers who bought other brands. Whereas all the other brands appeared to be capturing shoppers at retail or through expert and consumer reviews, this brand was dominating on social media, at events, and in alternative retail locations. We didn't have to look farther than Source Usage to tell our client right away that they had a massive problem coming.

Source Usage is powerful because it creates a picture of engagement in any given category while telling us where people are going for information, and where brands will have to play across an already wide array of marketing channels to be effective in selling their goods and services. Today, revealing this path to purchase is called shopper journey research. Shopper journey research, though, is often done through qualitative or ethnographic means. Our approach quantified the process. We don't really care in what order shoppers do their research and use their sources. That order seems important, but we attempted to map it out and found that there are so many possible combinations of what a shopper might do in what order that it's a waste of time because you can't get more than 6 percent of shoppers to do anything in remotely the same order. So let that linear kind of thinking go, because it isn't useful in informing your marketing strategy or other business decisions. It's not about the order they do it in. It's about how many of them do what. And later, which we'll get to, it's about how those sources influence the shopper.

We mentioned in our chapter on our Zero Moment of Truth research with Google that our Source Usage list started with dozens of sources across online, retail, word of mouth, TV and radio, print, and retail. Our Source Usage list has evolved as we stopped separating out mobile from other online activities (we found it doesn't matter to brands or shoppers if they do their search on a mobile device or laptop, but initially, when the technology was still evolving, it did) and as online retail media and social media sources have grown in number and usage.

Today our list sits at about 50 sources which we present to shoppers via a custom card sort method during an online survey. We ask Recent Purchasers which of these sources they used or came across before purchasing in a category. This is the question in the survey that often made old-school researchers (and survey programmers) worry. *That's such a long list! How will respondents manage?* We use a proprietary program design for this question that makes it very fast and intuitive for respondents. Because respondents are answering quickly, they are not pondering about what they may have done or could have done. This creates a "latency" component, which in our industry is considered more accurate. And the results for brands are incredibly useful because it tells them, in this age of increasing Shopper Promiscuity, where shoppers are turning for information and how it is shaping their decision making.

As experienced Brand Director Jon Harrington told us about the research work we did with him at a leading baby food brand:

> We had a fairly good understanding of the different communication channels and information sources that our consumers typically use, but the quantification of sources that we got from this research provided unique learnings. We became much better equipped to decide which communication channels required a mere

presence versus the channels we needed to fundamentally prioritize in order to be most impactful in our communications.

What Source Usage Tells Us Today

To best understand Source Usage and really illustrate why it's such a critical measure, let's look at it through a couple of different lenses. First, we'll examine some high-level trends related to Source Usage, then we'll dig into what it looks like when we break these findings up by key media channels that advertisers invest in. The data in Figure 5.1 is from the 2021 Shopper Influence Study we conducted across six different consumer categories and among 6,000 recent shoppers using the same methodology we have applied for clients like Google, Schwab, Pharmavite, Fortune Brands, and dozens of others.

Here's what we found. Shoppers are using more sources than ever before when making a purchase decision. Even for items like coffee or cleaning products, shoppers are using between 11 and 13 sources on average. For dog treats and supplements, it's about 14. For home furniture, it's about 17. And for home fitness equipment and self-improvement subscriptions like MasterClass or The Class by Taryn Toomey, it rockets up to over 24 and 31 sources, respectively.

FIGURE 5.1   Average number of sources used during the purchase journey by shoppers in each category as reported by the Alter Agents Shopper Influence Study, 2021

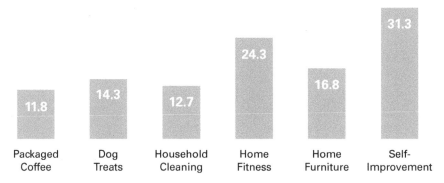

What we see here is that the fewest sources are used for packaged coffee (about 12) and highest average number for self-improvement subscriptions (about 31). What this means is that shoppers are voracious researchers. Most coffee drinkers are not bean juice connoisseurs, but they consult twelve different sources before deciding which coffee they'll buy and brew at home! And with access to information always available to shoppers via their mobile device, they are doing that research even when it's a relatively spontaneous purchase. But we also know that most purchases are planned and researched in advance, with 69 percent of total shoppers reporting that they researched their purchase. And 60 percent of shoppers say that they *always* research an item online before purchasing.

Even impulsive shoppers are not immune to planning and researching ahead of buying, with 52 percent of them saying they researched before they purchased—even if it was minutes before putting the product in their cart. Our research found little difference between the average number of sources used by Spontaneous Purchasers and Considered Purchasers (17 vs 19). Given this reality, brands have no choice but to operate from the position that every purchase decision is a considered one, and shoppers are hungry for information to make them feel confident before buying. If you don't think your customers are doing research before buying in your category, think again.

Eighty percent of shoppers are now using the internet as an information source before making a decision. Online sources are a huge driver of overall content being consumed by shoppers. With online sources now firmly entrenched in our decision, making process, brands must be prolific online content creators to ensure that shoppers find the information they need when they turn to product reviews, product specs, online videos, retailer websites, and other places for information. As retailers have recognized the revenue opportunity, they have also begun charging brands to speak to their online shoppers through banner ads, promoted products, and other media buys on the retailer's website. These online retail media sources have also seen significant increases in usage, further increasing the role of online sources in shopper decision making.

Younger shoppers, ecommerce shoppers, men, and higher income shoppers all do more research. Millennials use the most number of sources (23) while Boomers use the least (8) (Figure 5.2). Similarly, males use more sources (22) than females (15). Ecommerce shoppers use 25 sources on average while non-ecommerce shoppers use as few as 6. Those with above-average household income use a higher number of sources on average (23) while those with below-average household income use about 14 sources.

We've laid out some of the current picture as it relates to new shopper behavior norms. Now, let's see what that Source Usage looks like when we break these findings up by key media channels in which advertisers invest.

FIGURE 5.2   Average number of sources used during the purchase journey by shoppers in each generation as reported by the Alter Agents Shopper Influence study, 2021

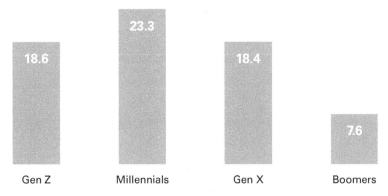

Online Sources Dominate

As we just highlighted from our 2021 study, 80 percent of shoppers are now using online sources before making a purchase decision across our range of categories. When we began this research in 2011, that figure stood at about 60 percent. But back then, all shoppers could do was basically search and hunt. The online source ecosystem wasn't as fully developed as it is today and digitally-native generations were just coming of age. Today, there are many more online sources and brands and retailers have gotten much more adept at engaging and guiding shoppers within these online experiences. Although a lot has changed in the past decade, online search was then and still is one of the most used sources of information for shoppers before making a purchase. Online consumer reviews have been among the most used online sources for a number of years with 56 percent of shoppers using online consumer reviews in their path to purchase. As you might expect, online sources have lower usage among lower cost, more frequently bought items such as coffee, dog supplements, and household cleaning products. However, "lower" is relative here. Even 36 percent of shoppers buying coffee are still using a search engine in their buying journey. And 26 percent of them are watching an online video about coffee, while 19 percent are reading about it in an online article or blog. Meanwhile, online sources for bigger ticket items such as home fitness equipment, furniture, and self-improvement subscriptions are off the charts. There is a near-ubiquitous use of online sources for shoppers before buying in one of these categories: it's

95 percent for home fitness equipment, 88 percent for furniture, and a whopping 98 percent for self-improvement subscriptions.

Online video also dominates as the fifth most-used online source at 48 percent average usage across our six categories. For a category such as home fitness purchases, above 70 percent of shoppers are watching a YouTube or other online video and these are among the top five most used sources for that category, while search engines (82 percent) and consumer reviews (79 percent) are the top two.

Clearly, online information sources have become a permanent part of the shopper decision, making process. And that makes sense—the internet is where the world's repository of information now lives, and shoppers know how to find the content they are looking for when they have unanswered questions.

Online Retail Media Has Exploded

Online retail channels have experienced the greatest transformation of all our sources since we began this work a decade ago. For a long time, retailer websites were not that sophisticated and shoppers continued to rely on search engines or consumer reviews to do the heavy lifting as it related to their research needs. However, retailers got savvy and realized that their websites are not only an important part of their owned media strategy— they could also generate revenue by selling brands space or targeting capabilities on those websites. Retailers like Amazon, Home Depot, Target, Walmart and others charge huge premiums for brands wishing to target website users. And those retailers are earning a good profit from it, with eMarketer finding that marketers spent $17.37 billion advertising on ecommerce sites and apps in 2020, up 38 percent from 2019 (Barr, 2020).

Retail media also works for shoppers. Increasingly, they rely on retailer or marketplace websites like Amazon to curate and guide their shopping experiences. Nearly half of all shoppers (47 percent) use online website recommendations like "Bestseller" or "Top Recommendations" to inform their purchase decisions. That percentage increases by 20 points for home fitness equipment or self-improvement subscriptions. Filtered searches on a retailer website or marketplace are also widely used, with over half of shoppers employing this technique in our higher ticket categories. For our CPG categories, the "most prominent featured products" options on retailer websites are used by a quarter of all shoppers.

Retail Still Plays an Important Role

A decade ago, retail sources were the most used sources for many categories. Today, while online sources have frequently surpassed in-store retail sources, brick-and-mortar retail is still widely used by shoppers, particularly for CPG categories such as coffee, pet treats and supplements, and household cleaning products. What's interesting is that, in many cases, retail usage has held steady over the past two years, despite a global pandemic that limited in-store shopping. And this happened despite the growth of online sources, meaning shoppers continued to rely on in-store sources to inform their purchases. The takeaway is that shoppers are not replacing one source with another. They're expanding their research. In-store signage and displays are used by about half of shoppers, at-shelf signage is used by 41 percent of shoppers, and endcaps are used by 35 percent of shoppers. Packaging also continues to play a critical role, with half of all shoppers using it as a resource when deciding on a purchase.

Social Media Makes a Mark

When we began doing this work, social media was still just emerging. Brands and retailers were using it to stay connected with consumers, but it wasn't really a place most folks were going for tactical shopper information. We had it on our Source Usage list, but it was usually an underperforming source. Over time, we began to see it inch up as shoppers began to rely on the internet to find reviews from other shoppers. Early on, YouTube became known by shoppers as a place for in-depth reviews and information that they seek out before making a purchase. And then, as platforms like Instagram, Pinterest, and Snapchat grew increasingly sophisticated, we began to see real shopper activity occurring in these spaces. Today, social media plays an increasingly powerful role in driving shopper decision-making. In a category like self-improvement subscription services, social media becomes a force multiplier. Shoppers are looking to Facebook (77 percent), Instagram (72 percent), social media influencers (70 percent) and YouTube (82 percent) before making their purchase. Even newcomer TikTok has quickly become a relatively widely used source for shoppers, with a quarter of them using the app before buying.

TV No Longer Dominates

TV actually did a bit better in our 2021 study than in years past, likely due to the increased viewership that we witnessed because of the Covid-19 pandemic, when consumers were spending more time at home and watching more television. Forty-five percent of shoppers used TV advertising to inform their purchase decision in our 2021 study—and TV's performance over indexes on usage for CPG categories. Its overall usage was highest among home fitness buyers and self-improvement subscription products. However, it will surprise no one that TV is not the dominant source for shoppers when making purchase decisions. With TV's impact no longer driving decision making among consumers and shoppers, increasingly ad budgets reflect this shift, with GroupM (2021) predicting TV ad spend will grow slowly at single digit rates, despite the increase in viewing time that occurred in 2021. TV will likely always be a go-to source for brands who want to generate awareness among large groups of consumers, but its reach advantage is slipping and it will need to work harder (beyond simple brand awareness tactics) to actually have shoppers use it as a source when considering buying in a category.

Word of Mouth Remains Critical

For decades, the recommendation of a friend or family member has been one of the fastest and most effective ways of informing a purchase decision. Whether it was your mother in-law's recommendation for a particular brand of cake mix, or your best friend's insistence you try a new workout class, word of mouth has for years been a relatively stable source for shoppers. We use it because it's reliable, easy, and trusted. And even the proliferation of online sources has not changed this, with 57 percent of shoppers using a family member or friend's recommendation before purchasing. Experts and store employees are also used by half of shoppers. So word of mouth matters, and even more so when these recommendations often come from someone you know and love via the constant connectedness of text messaging, social media, and other mobile channels. However, as we'll see when we get to our other key metric, Net Influence, as information has become widely accessible online, shoppers have grown more discerning about how much weight recommendations from family and friends have on their ultimate purchase decisions.

Audio is Evolving

We have a soft spot in our heart for audio. In part because it has been an underdog since online and social media sources began being seen as sexier than radio. Also because our own research shows that pound for pound, even when it generates lower Source Usage, its cost per thousand impressions (CPM) is often a good deal for advertisers. We also see that audio does a great job of converting shoppers. However, the big usage story in audio is that audio ads on streaming services like Spotify and Pandora and on podcasts have 30 percent and 23 percent usage across our six categories, respectively. While overall usage in this category isn't as high as other media types, for those who do listen, audio plays a key role that advertisers should not ignore.

Mobile Ubiquity

The big story in mobile is not that we're all attached to our phones. That's pretty obvious from the fact that the devices are basically extensions of our hands and our kids have started demanding we put them down. In fact, the ubiquity of mobile usage when researching products has meant that our team is now agnostic about whether shoppers are doing their research via their laptop or mobile device. Except from a user experience perspective, it doesn't really matter anymore which device the research is happening on. However, what is interesting is that half of shoppers are using retailers' mobile apps for their research. Our findings are consistent with research from Salesforce and Publicis. Sapient found that "71 percent of shoppers saying they use mobile devices in stores, a number that is up from 62 percent in 2017, and rises to 83 percent for consumers aged 18 to 44" (Alaimo, 2018).

This trend took years to gain traction after years of low engagement with those apps. Coupon or promotional discount apps like Ibotta also show relatively high Source Usage, with 40 percent of shoppers using them before buying.

Print still makes an impact

Print was a media source that was facing steep declines by the early aughts. But since then it has actually held relatively steady. Today, roughly two-thirds of all shoppers still use print media to inform their purchases, with

32 percent using magazine or newspaper ads, 32 percent relying on product reviews in magazines, 28 percent using product reviews in newspapers, and 33 percent using paper coupons. One print source that has been remarkably resilient is store circulars that highlight special products and sales, with 44 percent of all shoppers relying on this source to inform their purchases.

Everything Else!

The remaining sources are outdoor billboards, email marketing, direct physical mail, and in-game ads. These sources have between 20 and 34 percent usage among shoppers across all the categories we studied. However, generally these have all increased in usage over the years, in particular emails from brands or retailers or in-game ads, which were barely noticeable in the landscape but for a few forward-thinking brands. Home fitness and self-improvement subscriptions in particular are products that benefit from higher than average usage when it comes to emails or direct mail from brands or retailers and in-game ads.

As we've demonstrated, from this single question around Source Usage, we are learning so many things about shoppers—category engagement and consideration, media usage, earned vs paid media, and much more. Already we have rich insights to give our clients, but that is just the beginning. Usage is only half the story. In the next chapter, we'll look at our second key metric: Net Influence. Separately, these two sources are powerful in and of themselves. But when we put them together we get an unparalleled view of what really gets shoppers to *yes*.

KEY TAKEAWAYS

- Source Usage tells us which sources shoppers use along their path to purchase.

- Meeting your shoppers where they are requires understanding which sources they're using for information about your product.

- The more sources a shopper uses, the more research they are doing prior to purchase. The more research they are doing, the more invested they are in their decision.

References

Alaimo, D (2018) 87% of shoppers now begin product searches online, Retail Dive, August 15. www.retaildive.com/news/87-of-shoppers-now-begin-product-searches-online/530139/ (archived at https://perma.cc/EN3V-2XWV)

Barr, A (2020) Growth rate for ad spending on e-commerce sites will max out in 2020, eMarketer finds, Marketing Dive, October 23. www.marketingdive.com/news/growth-rate-for-ad-spending-on-e-commerce-sites-will-max-out-in-2020-emark/587627/ (archived at https://perma.cc/L3SK-BG6D)

GroupM (2021) This year next year: Global 2021 mid-year forecast, June 14. www.groupm.com/this-year-next-year-global-2021-mid-year-forecast/ (archived at https://perma.cc/WJ2B-YRY2)

06

Net Influence

Revealing the True ROI

Early on in our work together, we realized that we needed a metric that could lay bare not only whether a source was being used, but whether it actually had an impact. We knew the number of sources being used by shoppers was exploding (though we couldn't yet fully envision or understand just how massive that explosion would actually be) but we didn't have a way to say whether a particular source was really making a difference for shoppers.

Devora's boss at the IPG Media Lab and our design partner in this early work, John Ross, dubbed this missing metric "Influence." Before we get into influence, let's just stop for a moment to unpack its meaning. The word "influence" implies the ability—the power—to cause an effect through intangible means. Something or someone with influence doesn't need to command or use force to achieve a goal. The esteem in which it is held gives it power.

So influence in this scenario was about having the power to achieve the result that marketers like John wanted: get shoppers to say "yes" to a purchase. John had been a senior marketer at multiple retailers, including Home Depot where he had overseen one of the biggest and fastest expansions of a retailer in history with an ad budget that was in the hundreds of millions of dollars (Statista, 2021). If he could crack the code on what triggered shoppers to go from undecided to decided, he could accelerate his business exponentially. John had tons of money to throw at advertising, but was it effective?

John described to us how in every job he had, his core question was "What unlocks a shopper to say 'Yes' to a purchase?" Taking a look at the tools in his marketing toolkit, sifting through the big data and the qualitative research, he still felt that he was getting "mostly storytelling and anecdote." There was a lot of "what" information. What shoppers did, how they did it, etc. But very little on the "why" or the motivation behind the behavior.

Before his time at Home Depot, John had worked for a family retail business that later went public. They were buying other chains and then running them as their own business for a while. Then they'd run a "going out of business" sale, then rebrand, and then they'd open the other chains under their new name.

For a year or so John had the rare opportunity to be in control of two stores operating in the same market and selling the same products. Much like the origins of A/B testing in catalogues by Starch, John had markets he could manipulate in different ways and see how those manipulations changed shopper behavior. For market research, this is as close to scientific laboratory hypothesis testing as we can get.

John would max out spending on radio and TV, run a crazy sale, or try a new everyday low price (EDLP) strategy during that very precious time period where both stores were operating under the same model. It was a perfect test vs control market scenario and John's team was excited to dig into the data. Using multivariate regression analysis, they looked at the impacts of weather, holidays, and seasonality, in addition to these advertising changes. And yet the more scientific they got in their approach, the more they realized just how crude the tools to measure the marketing team's impact really were. Even in this nearly-ideal laboratory scenario, John's team could not reveal the impact of the advertising in a meaningful way.

This research was supplemented with many other methodologies—focus groups, phone surveys, credit card data, etc. He knew what shoppers were saying and what they were buying. But, even with all that data, it wasn't answering core questions that remained for him: *Why were shoppers buying? What was truly influencing them? What marketing or messaging made them say yes?*

Later, while he was at Home Depot running a campaign to sell a kitchen remodel to shoppers, the idea began to crystallize for him. John realized the ad he'd run today wasn't going to cause someone to go buy a kitchen tomorrow. That was a 24-month marketing cycle, and none of the marketing tools in existence were designed to measure a long decision-making cycle like that:

> How do I hold my agents accountable for the ROI of a magazine that won't have an effect for 24 months? I had to come up with something different than

just ROI, because the reporting year would be over before results came in. We'd conduct a focus group two years after the effort, and shoppers would show up with a folder filled with magazine clippings and ads that we ran. They'd say, "This was the picture that did it. I knew this was what we wanted." That would be the moment when we learned that the ads did influence shoppers and brought them to us, but not on the timetable that our tools measured.

John realized that shoppers had to overcome multiple decision barriers, or thresholds they needed to get over, in order to move to the next step down the path. He realized shoppers might be much more thoughtful than he was giving them credit for—or even than the shopper could articulate. He realized he needed a way to extract that sequence of events out of the narrative. John says it's similar to the way engineers diagnose problems:

> There's a problem with the very complex machine that is the marketing effort. You can't tear it apart and test every product, so you need a series of questionnaires. You need to be able to isolate pieces of the whole to identify what is working or not. Then, replace those systems and see if we solve the problem.

Ten or 20 years ago, marketers used TV, print, radio, traditional media, and maybe some billboards to get their message out. The number of things that an advertiser, even a deep-pocketed one, could do in order to influence shoppers was very narrow. As we've discussed, we're now in a new world with way more media types and advertisers are juggling all these new sources with varying degrees of reach, and with traditional media still in play.

What it means is that today a marketer's palette is really wide. It's like you had three colors to paint with in preschool, and now you're in college and you have a thousand colors at your disposal. How do you get the result that you want? In the past when you were dealing with mostly TV, radio, and print, a marketer could guess their way there by varying the amount of media they spent against it. *Let's plus up the radio and see what happens. Let's plus up TV.*

If you tried to do that today, you'd be retired before you got through all the permutations of bloggers, influencers, messaging apps, TikTok, online videos, and on and on. So the challenge has become even more sticky. Before, a marketer might have been able to afford TV, radio, and print. Maybe they'd give up some billboard spots in favor of direct mail. But back then a brand marketer with a decent budget could say "yes" to many things. That's impossible today. A marketer's budget would be spent way too soon. Now, marketers have got more choices, with more splintered audiences. On this basis alone, a marketer's ability to intuitively guess about what they are doing and what is actually working becomes much more difficult. John points out that there is a great irony for retailers:

> We sit on massive databases of information. Theoretically, if I'm a retailer with a hundred stores, I'd be able to just mine that database to learn what I need to know. I hired some analysts to run a big multivariate regression analysis on my sales data, but they'd come back and tell me the same answers that I got before. With that approach, we learned what caused people who already shop with us to buy more. The data wouldn't tell us how to attract new shoppers. So how do I track net new shoppers? How do I deal with anonymous shoppers who don't share their data with me?

While the data science, media analytics, and the number of choices and sophistication of our media outlets have improved, the complexity of trying to figure out which two or three levers can be pulled in order to drive incremental sales is staggering.

The Birth of Net Influence

John started working with Rebecca and Devora during this critical inflection point. He knew he could not get the answers he needed with traditional research, but if he could unlock those answers, he'd build a powerful research tool that gives marketers the knowledge and tactics to maximize their budgets and grow their businesses.

When John first explained his issues to Rebecca, she tried to respond with different tried and true methodologies—qualitative and quantitative, conjoint, MaxDiff, ethnographies, and shopalongs. No matter what she presented, John had seen it, tried it, and dismissed it. Rebecca began to connect the dots. John Ross, much like her primatologist mentor John Berard, was approaching things from an entirely different perspective. Rebecca had just begun her new business and realized she had a real opportunity to break the traditional rules of research and do something completely different. Devora's background in communications, marketing, and storytelling rounded out the picture. The three of them spent hours in conference rooms debating, scratching out notes on the whiteboard, and pushing ideas further.

The issue they tackled first was this idea of influence. What was actually influencing shoppers? The question is relatively easy. Did this piece of marketing influence your decision to buy this product? But to ask that question, you have to identify the right people and right context. So, the concept of influence created all of the other aspects of our research that turned out to be so original and powerful—talking to Recent Purchasers, asking them what they did instead of what they might do, and providing an expansive list of possible influence points.

Ultimately, we landed on Net Influence. The question is asked on a 1 to 10 scale for each source the shopper said they used. A "1" would mean that source had no influence on their decision to buy the product. A "10" would mean the source was highly influential in their final decision. Respondents were allowed to pick any number between 1 and 10.

Quickly, however, we realized showing a mean, median, or "top 3" box score (the sum of people who said 8, 9, or 10), would not tell the whole story. We found sources that were highly influential for some and not at all helpful for others. There were also sources that had a lot of responses hovering around the middle of the scale with few people on the more extreme ends. We needed one number to show all of this variation. The decision was made to apply a "net" methodology. Our score now shows the percentage of people who said a source was highly influential (8, 9, or 10 on the scale) minus the percentage of people who said the source was not influential (1, 2, or 3 on the scale). This allowed us to show one number, but incorporate the broader context of what the data was telling us.

How would a marketer use this information? Here's an example: if the research reveals that user reviews are highly influential, then retailers and brands can begin to direct shoppers to user reviews. They can increase the reviews' visibility on their website. They can give rewards to people who are writing those user reviews. They can put the user reviews on a digital sign in the aisle at the store. Suddenly the brand is doing a better job of influencing people who are already shopping. And to earn new shoppers? Now the marketer can go out and buy ads targeted at audiences of people who read consumer reviews.

The Tyranny of ROI

For a long time, ad agencies and marketing partners were very focused on proving ROI, or return on investment. As the data and tools had become more sophisticated, advertising buyers wanted to have a way to hold ad agencies more accountable for the money spent with them. Proving, mathematically, that the advertising was converting into X amount of dollars was highly appealing. The idea: how much return do you get back as a result of your advertising investments?

In the early days of advertising, when the analytics were weak, marketing teams and ad agencies used the fear of falling behind to get executives to increase the size of their ad budgets. *P&G is promoting heavily, therefore General Mills needs to go in and spend as much, and you've got to spend as much, at least! How do you expect to reach your audience?*

But as analytics started to improve, American businesses became more data-driven. Companies began making database-driven decisions in finance, then in merchandising, and later manufacturing. It's a reasonable evolution to say, "*Why can't I apply it to my marketing too?*" And out of that, brands began to call their advertising agencies and say, "*I have to hold you accountable for results and the easiest way to calculate that is through ROI. I gave you a million dollars to spend on advertising, how did that impact my sales?*"

All of a sudden the advertising agencies had to develop something new. They hired a lot more employees with data science skills. There was an explosion of media tech for agencies looking to prove that they were driving results. This caused a bit of an identity crisis for ad agencies. Used to being treated as brilliant creatives who used unconventional methods, they were now being asked to operate as a business division with a profit and loss statement and a clear demonstration that they were building the business. Some agencies tried their best to adapt and adjust while others tried to hold on to the *Mad Men* iconoclast status of the past.

In that turmoil, both the client and the advertising agency had to change. So they landed on ROI as a metric on which everyone could agree to disagree. John calls it "the tyranny of ROI" because, he says:

> It started for all the wrong reasons, so it feels hollow. Why is the tyranny of ROI ruling the advertising agency world? It's because ROI is this very thin metric that doesn't really reflect what causes sales to go up or down. If we gave the marketing team $1 million and our sales were worth $5 million, that's a great ROI. We'd celebrate. But was it the advertising that drove those incremental sales? Was it the quality of the product? A strong guarantee?

No one can say. So ROI, despite its promise to solve all woes, didn't close the loop either. Because it only told John and other people in his shoes what he was getting back based on everything he was doing. It didn't tell him whether there were new investments that were worth making. It didn't tell him what would get shoppers to act at greater rates of success, or what their needs were, or what would really make a difference for them. In other words, it didn't help him transform his budgets and advertising behaviors—it only helped him to maintain the status quo.

How Net Influence Works

That's why we developed Net Influence. Because with this simple metric, we can get a far more complete picture of human behavior. And now, with a lot less emotion, we can begin pulling the levers that move and drive results.

Think about all the times when you were considering buying something. Maybe you looked at a million sources. Maybe you thought about it for days or weeks or months. And then, you got a single recommendation from a single source and it made all the difference. Maybe it was your ride-or-die friend telling you that the workout class you'd been thinking about doing for $40 a month was changing her life. Maybe it was a review you read on Trip Advisor for a hotel just outside of your budget. Or maybe it was a guarantee on a car that took away that one last seed of doubt. Whatever it was, all the other stuff you were exposed to hadn't really moved you to buy until that one piece of messaging or content did the trick. And being able to bottle that, for marketers, is gold.

Net Influence became our North Star. The peanut butter to our Source Usage jelly. It opened up our eyes to a whole new world—one where we could say that while a lot of people use a source, it's not actually adding a lot of value. Or we could say that only 20 percent of people use another source, but it's incredibly influential. The data-driven stories we could generate for clients became far more dynamic and interesting. Because as we laid out in our prior chapter, there are lots of sources that get used. But just because a source was used doesn't mean it contributed to a decision to purchase. Net Influence solved for that. It told us what really made the difference for shoppers.

After defining Net Influence, we began to put the Source Usage and Net Influence data on a scatter plot. Source Usage data aligns along on the X axis, with Net Influence on the Y axis. Their intersection becomes the average that allows us to say, *this source is punching above its weight.* Or, *this one that you're spending a lot of money on is not really keeping up.*

An example of this was an early technology client who saw that their investment in Google search was paying off in the sense that many shoppers

FIGURE 6.1   The Value Quad Chart depicting how Net Influence and Source Usage are plotted to graphically show which sources are of most value

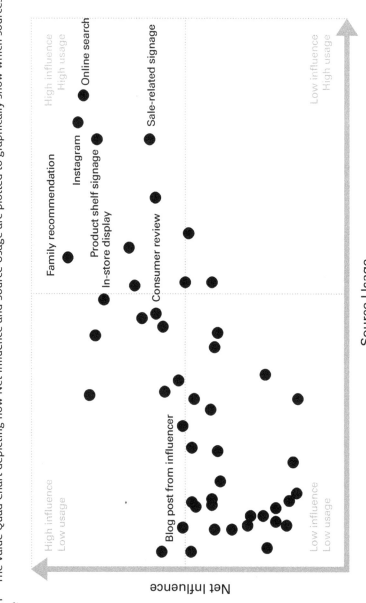

were using search before making a purchase decision. But search was actually lagging in terms of Net Influence. The CMO went to Google and said, "Hey, we're spending a lot with you, how can you make this search experience more influential for shoppers?" Out of that insight, Google developed a number of product improvements for the client which allowed their search investments to drive greater influence with shoppers.

Another financial services client uncovered that while shoppers looking for a new brokerage partner were using search, websites, and independent source rankings in their journey, the most used and most influential source was word of mouth: shoppers' financial advisors, consultants, spouses, and friends were all playing a critical role. The brand had known financial advisors were important, but they'd been uncertain on how far to go with their investments in driving word of mouth (which is admittedly harder than just programming a TV spot). But after our usage and influence findings came through, the brand decided to go all in. They began buying TV aimed at getting couples to talk about their investment decisions. They started promoting the kinds of conversations investors could take to their financial advisors. They created a series of public relations campaigns and paid advertisements that aimed to have their firm be recommended by financial advisors. That would not have been possible if they'd simply focused on ROI—the key to placing those bets with confidence was the magic of usage and influence.

As we shared earlier, initially we mapped out these findings using brightly colored heat maps, which provided some good theater in the beginning. But ultimately we landed on the quadrant charts as a way to reveal what and where clients should invest their dollars (Figure 6.2). Reading each quadrant was like unpacking a little story—what was in the upper right quadrant that was widely used and highly influential? Was it the sources the brands had invested mightily in? Or sources like packaging which barely got any love— and yet did all the heavy lifting? And what was up and coming in the upper left quadrant that wasn't as widely used but was highly influential? Social media, podcasts, radio were often to be found hanging out in that quadrant. The bottom right quadrant—high usage, low influence—this was the place where we often found TV—and, over time, Facebook. And the saddest corner, low usage and low influence—that's sometimes where clients had their ad dreams up-ended when they discovered sources they had invested so much money in were not up to the task (print was here for years—strangely, as it has become less available, today it's sometimes delivering greater influence; today TV is often found in this semi-tragic bottom left corner).

FIGURE 6.2   The inherent opportunities in the sections of the Value Quad Chart

Low usage and high influence	**High usage and high influence**
Sources that can be used to cater to specific groups effectively	Sources with highest opportunity
Low usage and low influence	**High usage and low influence**
Sources with lowest opportunity and where investments should be re-evaluated	Sources that can be mass invested in but where there is an opportunity to increase their impact

Net Influence in Today's Economy

Let's now take a look at how Net Influence is playing out across our six categories.

As you might imagine, not everyone finds the same sources useful. In our research, we find there are demographic and psychographic differences in perceptions of source influence. For example, men are more likely than women to find social media, audio, and TV sources influential. Millennials and Gen Xers are more likely to find word-of-mouth recommendations, online, print, mobile, and retail sources influential. And for Boomers, source influence is very low for social media, audio sources, online retail channels, and TV sources. Higher-income shoppers and eco-conscious shoppers are more likely to use sources and find them influential compared to their counterparts (lower-income shoppers and non-eco-conscious shoppers, respectively), indicating these two cohorts are more reliant on information sources to inform their decisions.

In our study of 6,000 US shoppers across six categories, we see generally, across all categories, that online, retail, and word of mouth rise to the top as the most used and most influential sources. However, as we drill down into the category and specific source used, we see significant shifts in terms of Net Influence. Let's look at how this plays out.

TABLE 6.1   Net Influence per source, as reported by principal gender categories

	Males	Females
Word-of-mouth recommendations	68.2% ↑	59.6%
Online general	65.9% ↑	54.5%
Social media	61.9% ↑	42.9%
Audio sources	61.8% ↑	37.5%
Print	61.0% ↑	52.2%
Mobile	60.7% ↑	52.4%
Retail	59.8% ↑	52.9%
Online retail channels	58.8% ↑	43.9%
Other information sources	58.4% ↑	39.8%
TV	54.2% ↑	35.5%

TABLE 6.2   Net Influence per source, as reported by generation categories

	Gen Z	Millennials	Gen X	Boomers
Word-of-mouth recommendations	53.1%	66.0%	69.8%	57.5%
Online general	48.8%	66.2%	62.3%	48.9%
Retail	43.1%	58.9%	61.7%	51.3%
Social media	39.4%	61.1%	55.1%	23.6%
Mobile	38.8%	59.9%	60.8%	53.7%
Print	37.5%	58.3%	62.6%	56.9%
Online retail channels	36.1%	59.4%	55.4%	30.3%
Audio sources	34.9%	58.6%	55.3%	21.1%
Other information sources	31.2%	56.2%	55.3%	32.4%
TV	27.6%	54.2%	49.3%	21.7%

Packaged Coffee

HIGH USAGE/HIGH INFLUENCE

In the packaged coffee category, product packaging, family/friend recommendations and signage at shelf all meet the high influence threshold for the category: about half of all shoppers use these sources, and half of all shoppers find them to be influential. That's good news in some respects—though if you're a coffee manufacturer, looking at what could increase the Net Influence of these sources (especially the two where shoppers find you at shelf) seems like a critical opportunity.

HIGH USAGE/LOW INFLUENCE

Meanwhile, in this high-frequency, CPG category search, signage in store and retailer mobile apps achieve higher Source Usage, but overall show less influence. TV, YouTube and Facebook also end up in the bottom right quadrant—likely owing to much of the content in this category being driven by traditional brand advertising instead of organic content that shoppers value.

LOW USAGE/HIGH INFLUENCE

Coupon and promotional apps as well as paper coupons are used in this category by about a third of shoppers—not enough to catapult it into the top right quadrant, but they demonstrate overall high influence, especially paper coupons and online expert review sites, which earn the highest influence in the category among all sources measured.

LOW USAGE/LOW INFLUENCE

In the coffee category the top "losers" for Net Influence are social media influencers, mobile ads, and magazine/newspaper ads. In and of itself, if we just looked at these results for the category we might assume this should inform our thinking for other categories, but as we'll see in a moment when we look at usage/influence beyond coffee, the shake out of Net Influence changes dramatically.

Our two other CPG categories—dog treats and household cleaning supplies—look similar to the coffee category, with some notable exceptions. In the dog treats category, shoppers place greater value on store employee recommendations and expert review sites (likely owing to dog owners not being able to ask their dogs which treat they'd prefer—and not being able (or willing) to judge for themselves which treats are best). And in the household cleaner category, shoppers are heavily influenced by paper coupons and coupon or promotional apps, which garner the highest influence of any source.

When we jump now to our remaining categories, home fitness equipment, home furniture and self-improvement subscriptions the influence story changes dramatically. Let's take a peek at home fitness equipment, which is one of our more interesting categories.

Home Fitness Equipment

HIGH USAGE/HIGH INFLUENCE

First, let's recall that overall online usage in this category sits at 95 percent. Let that sink in—almost 100 percent of shoppers in this category are using an online source before making a purchase. And among that ubiquity of shoppers, they rate online sources with 70 percent Net Influence. So online sources win the day overall, but the first, most used and most influential single source is consumer reviews. The second most used source and most influential source? YouTube. Followed by other online video sites. In this category, family and friend recommendations, which performed so well in our CPG categories, are 17 points lower than consumer reviews—even as they stand solidly in the high usage and high influence quadrant. But that tells us something about the relative influence of sources in this category— shoppers are looking for their own proof on review sites and video platforms and that is carrying greater weight than sources that often dominate influence, like word of mouth. Also, we see that, where social media influencers were in the low usage/low influence category for packaged coffee, here they are in the top right quadrant, with 51 percent of shoppers using them to inform their purchase and rating them with 64 percent Net Influence. Similarly, product reviews in magazines and Instagram make their first appearance in the upper right quadrant.

HIGH USAGE/LOW INFLUENCE

Search is also used with near ubiquity in this category, with 82 percent of shoppers using the source, but not as many shoppers (59 percent) finding it influential. Retailer website recommendations and apps as well as Facebook are also widely used but don't achieve the same level of influence that consumer reviews and videos do.

LOW USAGE/HIGH INFLUENCE

In our upper left quadrant in this category there are some meaningful surprises. First, chat app WhatsApp makes an appearance with 67 percent Net Influence. Over-the-air radio ads, podcasts, outdoor billboards, direct/postal mail from a brand or retailer and Snapchat also make an entry into this quadrant for the first time. What this tells us is that there are unexpected sources driving influence for shoppers in this category. These sources are likely often forgotten by brands—or certainly are lower on their list of priorities—and yet they are punching above their weight and probably worth considering for areas of investment.

Hopefully these data points have shown the nuance and power of Net Influence. It can drive so many business decisions and give marketers much more confidence in the ability to affect change at the register. When combined with Source Usage we develop a powerful tool that unlocks the mysteries of how shoppers are interacting with marketing.

KEY TAKEAWAYS

- Traditional research tools could not answer the simple question "What impact did this advertising have on a shopper's decision to buy?"

- By rethinking research to ask Recent Purchasers and have them take us step by step through their purchase process, we are able to directly ask that question. How influential was this source on your final decision to buy?

- Net Influence has proven to be a powerful tool, particularly when combined with Source Usage, by giving marketers a clear map of how advertising is interacting with other sources of information and where it is inspiring shoppers to act.

Reference

Statista (2021) Home Depot: Ad spend in the US 2012–2019, Statista. www.statista.com/statistics/298763/home-depot-ad-spending-usa/ (archived at https://perma.cc/7C8G-JDXG)

07

Other New Metrics for Guiding Decision Making

You can see from our prior chapter that Net Influence dramatically changes how we understand what's working and not working for shoppers in a given category or channel. But it isn't the whole picture. There are a few more key components to delivering a holistic view of what drives decision making for shoppers. The shopping decision is complex and can take a shopper in a multitude of very different directions.

To help us navigate this nuance more thoughtfully, we built a series of questions to reveal further insight into shoppers' decisions. In this chapter, we will cover three data topics that provide rich and compelling insights to our clients:

- **Source Content.** Beyond Source Usage and Net Influence, what were shoppers getting out of these sources? What information were they looking for and how does that change the way our clients use these sources?

- **Timeline.** How long did it take shoppers to go from undecided to decided? This not only illuminates the decision-making cycle, but also allows us to tease out the differences between impulsive shoppers and planners.

- **Barriers.** Shoppers often face small or large speed bumps on their way to purchasing something. We uncover what those challenges were and how easy it was for shoppers to overcome them so brands can take action to smooth the road.

Source Content

For a number of years, something called *360 degree marketing* promised the idea of a unified message across many points of customer contact. The idea was that brands should plaster their logo everywhere and have the same story across all channels. So wherever a consumer encountered them, they'd see a consistent story. This was nice in theory, and it does make sense that brands would want their brand to be in as many places as possible, represented consistently. However, as you might imagine, that also ends up looking a lot like Brand Narcissism and it's not really how shoppers think.

Shoppers use different sources to inform them on different areas of interest. For example, on social media they often look for reviews, word-of-mouth recommendations, and influencer opinions. Across retail sources, price is a key information focus. And for places like YouTube, they want in-depth product information. These are broad generalizations, but it is easy to see how different sources can encourage shoppers to seek different information. Billboards will not carry the same information as a three-minute ad read by your favorite podcaster. Shoppers understand this and use these sources differently to round out their overall information before making a decision. Understanding what information shoppers want from which sources is important for marketers for a few reasons.

Expectations

Shoppers are becoming more demanding by the day. A good experience with one purchase creates the expectation that the next purchase will be just as smooth. Think about the experience that Uber created for urbanites. While the company has many challenges and didn't really fulfill its promise outside of larger cities, the idea was a powerful one. Everything is done seamlessly on your phone. You can select a car to take you to your destination, set preferences if you're at a certain status, like music and conversation, and leave a tip and a review at the end. You don't have to share directions with the driver and they rarely wander down the wrong street. There's no transactional exchange of cash or credit card swiping. And they provide rapid connection to customer support if something goes wrong. For first time users, it feels luxe! Now compare that experience to what you get from public transportation in the United States.

Imagine a shopper stepping out of their Uber to shop at a store. At the store, they have to hunt down a sales associate for help, wait in a line, exchange money, and reject an offer to open up a store credit card. It's not a terrible experience, but it isn't exactly smooth. It involves a certain amount of interaction, friction, and exchange, and takes more time than walking right out of the store with the item after having purchased it on an app.

As we have seamless and positive experiences in some areas, our expectations increase for others. Shoppers think: *Why can't this store experience be as smooth as that other experience I had?* If a shopper found great information on a competitor's website, they would expect to find that same information on your website. When that expectation is not met, the experience turns negative for them.

Efficiency

It takes a lot of work to produce content across a dizzying array of marketing channels. Brands and their advertising partners spend a great deal of time and money putting together thoughtful content that is cohesive, true to the brand, and focused on shopper needs. But are they spending that money in the right places? Source Usage and Net Influence tell us the volume of activity around a source, but Source Content gives us insight into what shoppers are explicitly looking for from that source. This also ties into expectations. By understanding what people want from a source, you can meet their expectations and invest time and money effectively. A chart that comes out of Source Content is one of our least sexy graphs. It's literally a grid with check marks that tell what brands need to say in which contexts. Brand marketers have told us they reference this chart as they are plotting their messaging strategy. Now, they have a road map of what to say and where.

Expansion

We always enjoy it when clients are surprised by the data we deliver, and this happens with Source Content more than we would have thought. Inevitably, someone in the room will remark that they would have never thought shoppers were looking at one particular source for a specific piece of information. This allows the brand to identify marketing channels or touchpoints where they may never have thought to expand into. We hear this a lot about the role that YouTube plays in educating shoppers deeply on a particular product or feature. We've seen numerous examples where clients have used Source Content to identify that previously untouched channels such as podcasts, in-store circulars, or messaging apps like Snapchat and WhatsApp are serving as educational sources or are where shoppers are trading opinions on product details.

CASE STUDY
Cake Mix

Let's come back to the example of cake mix that we discussed in Chapter 1 to look at an example of how Source Content can be used effectively to increase a brand's Net Influence scores. We used cake mix as an example in an early prototype of this work for years. At the time, the category was suffering from an unhealthy reliance on price and promotions to move its product. Across all brands, the boxes all looked alike and used similar words like "moist" (which was subsequently on the world's worst words list for several years in a row) and featured slices of... you guessed it, a slice of moist looking cake! Despite our insights revealing that shoppers were looking at Source Content for creative ideas and confidence, none of these brands were using their paid, owned, or earned advertising channels to provide content addressing either of these needs. Sure, there were a few recipes listed on the brand website or consumer reviews on their Facebook page, but overall there was no content strategy at all that actually spoke to shoppers' desired areas of interest.

Today, cake mix brands have become increasingly more effective content creators. Their websites feature tips and tricks, recipes for every celebration from birthdays to Pride, high-quality photos, and links to Pinterest, Instagram, and Twitter. Their boxes now feature ideas for ingredient swaps and quick ways to change the texture and flavor of the cake by adding an extra egg or topping with m&ms. There are still opportunities where we'd love to slide over these findings to the CMO of Betty Crocker and say, "Add more opportunities for home bakers to take on creativity challenges," or "Don't forget the moms and dads who need a little more confidence to take on a baking project." But that's the ideal role of Source Content—it helps brands understand what content will make their sources more influential by providing the information that matters most to shoppers.

Packaged Coffee Shoppers and Source Content

For a look at how Source Content plays out by category, let's look at the packaged coffee category again and which sources shoppers are using for which types of content. Table 7.1 shows the percentage of shoppers in the category that expected these sources to contain consumer reviews.

It's fascinating here that social media influencers are the number one source of consumer reviews content. It makes sense that shoppers would turn to social media sources for reviews, but what we find incredible is that seeking out reviews is now primarily done online—over the word of mouth of your friend or family member.

TABLE 7.1   Share of Packaged Coffee Shoppers who turn to a source for consumer reviews

Social media influencers	53%
Online articles or blogs (e.g., cooking, sustainability, coffee enthusiast blogs)	49%
YouTube	46%
Online discussion forums (e.g., Reddit)	45%
Product reviews in magazines	45%

This list gives us a sense of the places that shoppers trust for reviews on the products they buy—if they didn't trust the sources, they wouldn't consult them. YouTube has also become a de facto source for review content, on par with product reviews in magazines, which were a staple of consumer life for decades. Welcome to the digital era!

Shoppers know exactly where to go for pricing information—whether they are shopping online or at retail (Table 7.2). Pricing and promotional Source Content plays out about how we might expect; however, it's amazing to see digital coupon sources like promotional apps or online coupons now ahead of paper coupons for this content. Store circulars have also been a remarkably resilient legacy channel, with shoppers relying on these even more than at-shelf signage and displays.

TABLE 7.2   Share of Packaged Coffee Shoppers who turn to a source to learn about prices or promotions

Coupon or promotional discount app	69%
Online coupon	68%
Paper coupon	66%
Store circulars that highlight special products and sales	66%
Signage and displays in store	63%
Signage at shelf	61%

Shoppers are turning to both the package itself and professional or friend and family recommendations for details about the product (Table 7.3). They are comparing the brand's claims against the real-life experiences of people they know or online consumer reviews from strangers. Shoppers have always crowdsourced information on a product rather than solely relying on the brand's own claims. But it is extraordinary to note the extent to which "most prominent featured products" on sites like Amazon have become a go-to source for product attributes.

TABLE 7.3   Share of Packaged Coffee Shoppers who turn to a source to learn about product attributes, like the level of roast, fineness of grind, or procurement source

Packaging or photos of product packaging (e.g., labels, ingredients, description, etc.)	56%
Professional/expert recommendations	43%
Family member or friend's recommendation	42%
Most prominent featured products on online marketplaces	40%
Online expert review sites	37%
Magazine/newspaper ads	35%

Shoppers look to store employee recommendations, at-shelf reviews, and packaging for information about product functions (Table 7.4). However, they also trade details with friends and family about product functions on the private messaging app WhatsApp. Here, too, shoppers acknowledge the role filtered search on online retail marketplaces like Amazon play in providing critical content to them about the products in which they are interested.

TABLE 7.4   Share of Packaged Coffee Shoppers who turn to a source to learn about product functions, like whether it's best for use in espresso, americanos or cappuccinos, or to be used in coffee cakes

Store employees' recommendations	27%
At-shelf reviews	26%
Packaging or photos of product packaging (e.g., labels, ingredients)	25%
WhatsApp	24%
Professional/expert recommendations	24%
Online marketplace filtered search (e.g., price, categorical, features)	24%

If you're a coffee or CPG brand, these insights become programming guidelines, and suddenly it becomes easier to figure out what to say and where to focus. Now you know that influencers are a critical part of your review strategy. And that online reviews have to be a priority. You also see that paper coupons are still in play, but that you'll have to play in digital coupons as well. You know now that your packaging has to do a lot of heavy lifting—both on the actual package as well as in the photos of the package that take the place of the actual package when shoppers are looking at making a purchase online. And, finally, you see that shoppers are seeking information about product functions from a variety of sources including at-shelf reviews, product packaging and even WhatsApp. You can prioritize information sharing and education of your product because it's clear shoppers are interested in knowing more.

Home Fitness Equipment Shoppers and Source Content

Now let's look at another category: home fitness equipment. How does it compare to the types of content shoppers are seeking out from which sources?

If you're a home fitness equipment brand, knowing that your search and YouTube strategy should include links to reviews is a key strategic advantage. It's not just about getting found in search—it's about ensuring shoppers are seeing the reviews that will give them the confidence to purchase (Table 7.5).

TABLE 7.5   Share of Home Fitness Equipment Shoppers who turn to a source to find consumer reviews, like those by fitness bloggers, or health and wellness influencer endorsements

Search engine (e.g., Google, Yahoo, etc.)	45%
YouTube	44%
Social media influencers	44%
Online expert review sites	44%
Facebook	44%

For home fitness equipment, it plays out similarly to the coffee category in terms of pricing and promotions (Table 7.6). But here we see that retailer mobile apps and online marketplace filtered search play a role. This offers brands a clear directive about where and how to place promotions that will be effective.

TABLE 7.6   Share of Home Fitness Equipment Shoppers who turn to a source to learn about price and promotions, like holiday sales and discount codes at fitness equipment companies

Coupon or promotional discount app	52%
Signage at shelf	51%
Online coupon	49%
Signage and displays in store	48%
Retailer mobile app (e.g., Target, Walmart app)	48%
Online marketplace filtered search	46%

Search also plays a role in helping connect shoppers to information about product attributes (Table 7.7). So a home equipment brand can program their search strategy to include reviews and product details. We also see here direct mail from a retailer or brand playing a role in educating shoppers about product attributes—something that could have been easily forgotten on the cutting room floor with all the other tactics a marketer today must pursue.

TABLE 7.7   Share of Home Fitness Equipment Shoppers who turn to a source to learn about product attributes, like motorization, tracking ability, resistance offering, impact intensity, automation level, or the ease of setting up the equipment

Search engine (e.g., Google, Yahoo, etc.)	40%
Family member or friend's recommendation	40%
YouTube	40%
Professional/expert recommendations	40%
Direct/postal mail from a brand or retailer	39%
Packaging or photos of product packaging (e.g., labels, description, etc.)	38%

Finally, we see shoppers turning heavily to YouTube and other online videos for product function information (Table 7.8). This is a great opportunity for a brand marketer looking at this data to invest in an organic content strategy on some of these online video platforms—and again, this might never have been revealed without Source Content as a key metric.

TABLE 7.8   Share of Home Fitness Equipment Shoppers who turn to a source to learn about product functions, like which is best to use for competitive training, weight training, or generic at-home workout routines to stay fit

YouTube	33%
Professional/expert recommendations	30%
Online video (e.g., YouTube, Vimeo, Facebook video, vlogs, etc.)	29%
Search engine (e.g., Google, Yahoo, etc.)	28%
Online chat feature on retailer website	27%
Packaging or photos of product packaging (e.g., labels, ingredients, description, etc.)	26%

Once brands understand what types of content shoppers want from sources, it gets much easier to behave in ways that fight off the inclination towards Brand Narcissism. Paying attention to Source Content allows brands to get over themselves and connect with shoppers—what do they want to know? What are they thinking about? And when we do this, it also gets easier to be a marketer. Now you don't have to guess, you know what to say, where, and to whom.

Timeline

Another key component of our methodology is understanding how time informs the shopper's decision-making process. How long does it take for shoppers to go from undecided to decided? This is the decision timeline. When presenting our research to a client, this is where we start. The timeline creates context for our clients that frames the rest of the data. It's a critical measure to set up our findings, because it orients us around how the decision in a particular category gets made. It makes sense—time gives us a picture of how thoughtful shoppers are being, how long it takes them to feel confident, and similar to Source Usage, it's a proxy for consideration. The timeline was a particular area of this research where shoppers always surprised us. No matter the category, we were often proven wrong when we predicted how long the majority of shoppers actually needed to make a purchase decision.

One example of where we've seen the timeline surprise us is the automotive category, discussed in earlier chapters. We might assume that shoppers buying a car might need weeks or months to decide. And it's true, many do take their time with such an important decision. However, our research has shown for years that 15 percent of shoppers make the decision from start to finish within a week or less. And that's not just rich guys who decide to buy a convertible on a whim. It's shoppers who have crashed their car in an accident, or have a new job, or are about to bring a new baby into the household. Or, they are like Rebecca, who hates taking a long time to make a decision and will pull the trigger on a new car after a day or two of research and a test drive. What's amazing about the length of time of the shopper journey is that it always requires us to re-examine our assumptions about the purchase journey.

Another important distinction with the timeline is that shoppers can sometimes use a lot of sources over a long period of time, or they can use a lot of sources in a short period. When we did research into motor oil for a large conglomerate a number of years ago, we conducted the work in China, Russia, and the United States. We found that in China shoppers had a much shorter timeline to purchase—but they used far more sources. In Russia, the timeline was quite long, but fewer sources were used overall. Americans were right in the middle. This began to show us that different things could compel shoppers to extend or shorten their purchase timeline that we had not anticipated—for example, culture, context, or the category itself.

Generally, as information has become easier for shoppers to access, we've seen shopper decision timelines decrease. But the number of sources people use during that time has consistently increased. This tells us that shoppers have become very adept and comfortable researchers—they know they can easily find the information they are looking for and are undaunted in the face of infinite sources to inform their decision. They can relax a little, look at reviews, check out websites, poke around on social media and they'll be able to make their purchase with confidence. Across all our categories, the majority of shoppers make their decision within a day. However, 43 percent take two days to four weeks. Figure 7.1 shows how that looks by category.

FIGURE 7.1 Share of shoppers by category who complete purchases within a specified time frame

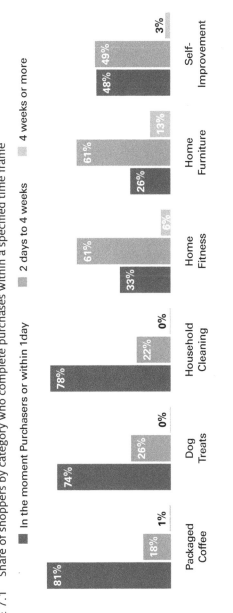

- In the moment Purchasers or within 1day
- 2 days to 4 weeks
- 4 weeks or more

Packaged Coffee: 81%, 18%, 1%

Dog Treats: 74%, 26%, 0%

Household Cleaning: 78%, 22%, 0%

Home Fitness: 33%, 61%, 6%

Home Furniture: 26%, 61%, 13%

Self-Improvement: 48%, 49%, 3%

To recap, the timeline can vary and isn't necessarily proportional to the number of sources used. Let's look now at which sources get used *when* shoppers are on the journey.

As shoppers get closer to purchase, they start to accelerate the number of sources they are using. Here, the numbers in brackets denote the mean timeline score (between 1 to 10, where 10 is "when I finally made the purchase" and 1 is "when I first started thinking about the purchase." Search engine (5.94) is used early on in the shopping process in the consideration phase, when shoppers are just getting acquainted with the product or category and are looking to find more information as they embark on their shopping journey. TV advertising is almost always used earlier on in the process (6.21)—which, instinctively, given how it's been traditionally used to raise brand awareness, makes sense. Other online sources such as consumer reviews (6.40), online expert review sites (6.54) and online videos (6.52) are still used when considering the purchase, but slightly after search engine usage.

Among social media platforms, Snapchat (7.00) and WhatsApp (7.18) are used somewhat closer to purchase (likely because these function more as messaging apps) whereas Instagram (6.77), Facebook (6.53), and YouTube (6.47) are used comparatively earlier on.

Retail sources like in-store signage and retailer websites, as we might expect, are used closer to purchase. Online coupon (7.02) and online chat feature on website (7.01) are also used closer to purchase. This makes sense since online coupons would be applied directly at checkout in an online purchase while website chat features are possibly used to provide assistance closer to when making the purchase.

In-store sources such as store employee recommendations (7.04), signage at shelf (6.96) and signage and displays in store (6.76) are unsurprisingly used closer to the purchase, as they directly influence the touchpoints a shopper interacts with typically right before making an in-store purchase. Across gender and generations, the actual time spent thinking about a purchase is relatively similar. This tells us that category is a more critical driver of the purchase timeline than demographic differences. However, there are some shopper attitudes that vary by generation and differentiate Gen Z and Millennials from Boomers (Table 7.9), and by gender (Table 7.10).

Timeline as a metric provides a critical view into what it takes for shoppers to say "*Yes.*" It gives us insight into how complex a category is and helps reveal how brands should think about the decision timeline in their category. For example, a brand that sells products during the Back to School

TABLE 7.9   Share of shoppers agreeing with the statement, by generation

Statement	Gen Z/ Millennials	Boomers
I'm always scrambling to find the items I need	34% ↑	13%
I typically go into a store/site knowing exactly what I want	47%	54% ↑
Most of my purchases are planned	61%	86% ↑

TABLE 7.10   Share of shoppers agreeing with the statement, by principal gender category

Statement	Males	Females
I'm always scrambling to find the items I need	32% ↑	25%
Most of my purchases are planned	67%	70% ↑

season may think the month prior to school starting is the ideal time to promote their products. But it may be that shopper's research begins even sooner, despite the price of the item being under $20. Alternatively, home fitness brands may know their products require greater consideration, which could span several weeks—and yet, for the bulk of shoppers, the actual decision happens in a much shorter time frame, requiring a different kind of messaging and content to get shoppers ready to purchase.

Barriers to Purchase

The last area we will explore in this chapter is the barriers to purchase—what gets in the way of shoppers making a final decision? While leading a workshop at the IPG Media Lab with a group of executives from a major automotive brand, Devora will never forget the hubris she experienced from one of the leading members of the brand's marketing team. She was explaining how our approach to barriers works and he said, "We know all the barriers to buying a car. Brand and Price. That's it."

Really, she thought. *Brand and price. Huh. For the car that's going to drive your newborn home from the hospital. For the car that some consider to be a critical status symbol. For the car that they view as a way to do their part for the environment. Right.* Devora knew from recent research that shoppers were dealing with a number of barriers that were far more extensive than brand and price. The marketing executive might have known many things, but his instincts here were wrong.

This goes right back to the Brand Narcissism that so permeates insights. Brand and price are two things that are, ostensibly, under the control of brand managers and advertisers. If those things are barriers, brand managers and advertisers can adjust them. Naturally, we want to understand how shoppers are experiencing the things we have control over, but it does not reflect the shoppers' experience. Yes, brand and price are barriers, but there are so many nuances within those two broad categories, plus a host of other barriers that we need to explore. Here are some examples:

- Lack of clarity or sufficient information about product attributes
- Lack of confidence about how the product will work
- Difficulty assessing the quality of a product
- Concerns about fraudulent products
- Inability to obtain customer support
- Unavailability of the item within the required time frame
- Concerns regarding company or brand's credibility
- Perceptions of the cost or items actually being too expensive
- Lack of a promotional offer or coupon
- Concerns about ethical sourcing or manufacturing
- How others perceive the product, service, or brand

When we dig into barriers, a motivating question for us is: are there barriers that we may not have imagined before that are stopping people from buying? Because of this, we like to get exhaustive with our list of barriers. Similar to putting Source Usage and Net Influence together, our approach on barriers isn't only to ask what stops shoppers. We also want to understand which barriers they can actually overcome. Because sometimes there are things that could stop shoppers from buying, but which they can get over pretty easily. To quantify the barriers and reveal which of them can be more easily addressed than others, we ask a two-part question.

First, we ask Recent Purchasers which barriers popped up for them during their decision process that may have stopped them along the way. Again, this list of barriers is comprehensive and includes both those the brand may anticipate and ones that may seem insignificant. Next, after respondents have selected which barriers were an issue for them (most shoppers face around three, on average) we ask them to rate the level of difficulty they had in overcoming that barrier. Some, like price, can be easily overcome with a coupon, sale, or promotion. Others, like lack of availability of the product a shopper wants, could be much harder to overcome. What results from this process is an actionable way for brands to learn what can stop shoppers from buying and how to prioritize their response to those barriers. We often discuss low-hanging fruit fixes with clients. This is a group of barriers that get in the way of purchase decisions, but that the brand could quickly resolve—not enough information on the website, for example. Even if a barrier only affected five percent of the population, imagine what converting that five percent can mean for bottom line sales. If your brand removes a barrier that exists for other brands in the category, that five percent of shoppers are yours for the taking.

Another area to explore are those barriers that are very difficult to overcome. Are a lot of people affected by them? What brands did shoppers impacted by these difficult barriers ultimately buy? What does that tell us about those brands' abilities to resolve that barrier? By digging into the data, we can find several immediate paths to improved sales performance. For the brands willing to do what it takes, it can be a game-changing way to address shopper concerns.

Here's an example. We uncovered a massive barrier in the decision-making process for a financial services client. Nearly 80 percent of shoppers named "Meeting with the broker" as a barrier to making their final decision. This barrier appeared at both the beginning and end of their shopping journey. They knew they had to have the conversation, but a fear of heavy-handed sales tactics and double talk made the prospect of the meeting a strong deterrent. While they were researching brokerage firms, conversations with a broker were essential. But shoppers would often put off the meeting or delay entering into the shopping process simply out of anxiety about this conversation.

When we met with our client and presented that finding, we had a great brainstorm about easier access points for shoppers that would take some of the pressure off of the broker experience. They also retooled their sales training, changed their messaging to talk about their supportive and friendly brokers, and instituted more frequent customer feedback. These weren't easy changes for the organization to make, but they made a big difference to their bottom line as their reputation grew, word-of-mouth recommendations spread, and customers learned about the superior experience our client offered.

Barriers can also differ depending on the specific shopper's context. Shoppers that take longer to make their decisions often encounter more barriers. This could be because they are being more thorough or because they are more anxious about the decision. A higher percentage of ecommerce shoppers face barriers, as the user experience, inability to examine the item in person, and overwhelming choices make that purchase channel more fraught. Understanding how different sub-groups are impacted by barriers further enhances the brand's opportunity to effectively target and convert shoppers.

The Shopper Influence data is rich and we could go on, quite happily, with more examples and illustrations. By looking at the shopper's experience from their point of view, while their actions are still fresh in their memory, we can reveal powerful insights that fundamentally change the way brands operate. We have seen it time and again in our business and still remain amazed with how transformative these insights can be.

KEY TAKEAWAYS

- Source Usage and Net Influence describe the power of a source in impacting shopper decisions, but we must also understand what content they were seeking from which sources. By exploring what information people were looking for, we can place the right content in their hands at the right time.

- The shopping journey is not linear, but shoppers can tell you roughly when they took certain actions—at the beginning, middle, or end of the decision-making process. This timeline illuminates key insights on how long shoppers are considering their purchase and what sources they use at which points.

- Digging into barriers rounds out the shopper's story. When speed bumps are encountered, how hard were they to overcome? What are the potential pitfalls?

08

Redefining Brand Tracking

Over these last few chapters, we have shared with you dozens of compelling insights that would lead brand managers, marketers, and product development teams to create real change. By talking to Recent Purchasers, our data reveals specific tactics brands can use to gain market share. Rather than operating in the hypothetical, our data is grounded in real shopper behavior. We hear consistently from our clients that our data leads to meaningful internal action and change. As researchers, this is both gratifying and motivating. If only all projects could be this fulfilling.

Brand Tracking: Necessary, but Frustrating

We have worked on everything from segmentations and conjoint analyses to MaxDiffs and brand tracking. All of these projects have their functions and all of them have yielded interesting results that satisfy clients. Except for one: brand tracking. It is rare to find the research buyer or the research supplier that wakes up in the morning excited to work on brand tracking research. Why is that? Any good market research professor would tell you that brand tracking is essential to understanding the voice of the consumer and helping brands navigate the competitive marketplace. Every textbook, every account planner, and every brand manager all consider brand tracking to be necessary. The companies that do not have a brand tracker, most likely for budgetary reasons, are anxiously awaiting the day when they can finally fund the research.

The reason for this entrenched belief goes back to the early days of market research with Starch and Gallup. Brand tracking research is built to measure the consideration to purchase funnel. Remember our old friends, the metrics of awareness, familiarity, consideration, and purchase intent? The latest addition to this family of metrics is the Net Promoter Score. Our industry has been working with these metrics in some way for almost a century. We think if you were to ask any research buyer or provider, they would tell you that they find brand tracking to be frustrating. But most feel they would have a difficult time articulating why. They believe it is essential, but they find both the process and the results of brand tracking research to be fundamentally frustrating.

One of the hardest things to do as a market researcher is to write a new headline on a monthly report for a continuous tracker. When the numbers haven't moved, or when the story is the same, or when there are no new insights, how do you find something interesting and compelling to put on the page for your client?

Let's look at this from the research buyer's side as well. Tracking studies are extremely expensive. Whether it is wave or continuous tracking, the cost is high and in most organizations, the tracking study is the largest project in their research budget. Companies not only invest in this tracking research financially, but they invest in it emotionally as well. Many companies have based bonuses and salary increases on whether the metrics from their brand tracking study show desired results. CEOs will receive highlight reports of brand tracking data, and then rattle their team with hard questions if the numbers aren't moving.

On both the buyer's and provider's side, tracking metrics can be slow to move, difficult to extract meaningful insights from, and ultimately frustrating. Too many times, we have seen tracking data received and then filed away by the client team because there isn't much to do with it—the numbers are the same as they were last time. In other cases, all of this research, effort, and money is boiled down to a single infographic, page, or even just one number that the leadership at the company is most interested in.

Whenever a tracking project begins, both the provider team and the buyer team are full of hope and excitement for what they are building. Multiple conversations with stakeholders lead to a thoughtful and thorough questionnaire that addresses all of the clients' concerns while incorporating the best practices that the agency brings to their work. The first reports to come in are met with anticipation, the conference room is full when the data is presented, and there is a vigorous and engaged debate over the findings.

But a year or two later, the conference room is nearly empty. Attendees aren't looking forward to the numbers. They are sending emails or reading other material during the presentation. The healthy and invigorating debates that happened in the past have turned into mumbled *thank-yous* and *goodbyes* and *see you next months* as the clients quickly file out the door. It's hard to keep a room of people engaged and interested when the data doesn't change and there are no new results.

This is a pretty dire scenario. Unfortunately, it is not uncommon. Whenever we talk to clients or our colleagues in other agencies or research suppliers, we all knowingly snicker and roll our eyes when sharing stories of how tracking research has become frustrating or mundane, or is leading to staff burnout and unhappiness. But what is to be done about it? If we hold the purchase funnel as sacrosanct, then nothing can be done about it. We can keep hoping for a tweak or an adjustment or some other unknown miracle that will turn this very necessary research into something more. Some clients think starting over with a new agency and some new thinking will generate different results. But we still find ourselves in sparsely populated conference rooms with disengaged clients.

Despite this bleak situation, we have never lost the belief that tracking can and should be a meaningful and useful part of a researcher's toolkit. We do need to understand how consumers are thinking, what they are doing, and why they are doing it. So, how do we fix this problem?

Narcissism and the Purchase Funnel

In our chapter on Brand Narcissism, we talked about how tracking metrics are flawed. The questions that define the purchase funnel are narcissistic. They are questions that the marketers and brand managers want to be answered but they do not reflect the shoppers' experience. What are the non-narcissistic ways of asking those questions? Our team has grappled with this for a very long time. We've held tightly to the belief that if we could redefine these questions and show people something analogous, but shopper-focused, we would open up a whole new world of powerful brand tracking insights.

Perhaps we could ask about *consideration* from the point of view of the shopper. But how could we reframe these questions in a way that makes sense for the shoppers' experience? Let's take a look at consideration, which we get at by asking the question, "Which of the following brands would you consider the next time you buy in this category?" That is a narcissistic question. Shoppers don't think in terms of a consideration set of brands when they begin their shopping journey. However, it is quite challenging to think of a way to reframe that question from a shopper's perspective. What we've come to realize over time and over many exercises trying to reframe these questions is that it doesn't work because the premise of the purchase funnel is the ultimate error in this formula. The purchase funnel is built on assumptions that people make about what they will do in the future. But we have learned over the last decade that people are not able to connect what they think they will do in the future with what they actually do. This is because, in our unbound economy, the choices are so vast that the ability to predict behavior is diluted past the point of utility.

Thinking back to the mid-1960s when market research hit its scientific stride, shoppers were still operating in a very constrained, narrow environment. As we've discussed before, the distribution channels were limited, the brands on the shelf were limited, and a retail store or mail-order catalogs were your primary options for purchase. In that ecosystem, the concept of the purchase funnel worked. Well, sort of. Because shoppers had limited choice it was easier for their assumptions about their future behavior to stay relatively true to their actions.

In today's unconstrained world filled with promiscuous shoppers, the purchase funnel starts to break down. Today, nothing is linear when it comes to shoppers, their behaviors, and the decisions they make. There are so many different factors, influences, purchase channels, brands, and disruptors that the same person can shop drastically differently from one category to the next or from one day to the next in the very same category. This means hypothetical research like brand tracking ultimately fails because with so many options in front of us we can't predict exactly how we're going to behave in the marketplace at the time.

Rejecting the Traditional Brand Tracker

Now, let's pause here for a moment because the second half of this chapter is going to seem a bit radical. We want to acknowledge that we have spent many years doing traditional brand tracking research. We work hard with our clients to develop the smartest tracking research that we can, to deliver the most compelling insights possible, and try to keep the tracking research as fresh and meaningful as possible—exactly like every other researcher. If you are in this industry, you know we all have the same goals of creating excellent research to give our clients meaningful insights. Our aim is not to mock our past research or to dismiss any of the hard work or excellent thinking that has gone into brand tracking design. We have all been trying to make the best of this methodology. But we also believe there is mounting evidence that brand tracking has lost its relevance. And we believe we need to wholly redesign the research from scratch.

Where does that leave us? The only way that shoppers can answer the purchase funnel questions is in the hypothetical context. But we know that hypothetical doesn't translate to real-world behaviors. What we have seen time and time again in our Shopper Influence research is that talking to Recent Purchasers who give you facts about what they have done is much more powerful and revealing than hypothetical questions. That leaves us with only one conclusion: we must entirely rebuild our concept of brand tracking, take it away from a hypothetical and put it to a cohort of actual purchasers.

After wrestling with this issue ourselves for many years, we came to a rather startling and simple conclusion: the purchase funnel no longer makes sense. It does not connect with actual shoppers' behavior. It does not represent the typical shopper, because there is none. As researchers with decades of experience, the idea of turning our backs on the purchase funnel is quite scary. But if we don't acknowledge that the purchase funnel is broken, then we can never build something better.

So what does brand tracking look like if there is no purchase funnel to guide it? We tried very hard to come up with new questions or ways to ask things that could be seen as surrogates for our existing funnel metrics. But no matter how we theorized and strategized and invented, nothing felt right. That's when it dawned on us. The answer to the problem with brand tracking wasn't about modifying brand tracking but walking away from it entirely and designing actionable research. In our experience, that actionable tool is Shopper Influence research.

While the purchase funnel questions might not have an analogous counterpart in our Shopper Influence research, the questions that brands and marketers want answered from tracking research do. To illustrate how Shopper Influence research can be used to supplant brand tracking, let's take each of these questions in turn.

What Do People Think of My Brand?

In brand tracking, this is answered not only with the purchase funnel, but also with metrics like imagery and personality batteries. In these questions, respondents are asked to align different types of statements with the client's brand and key competitors. These could be statements like "Is trustworthy," "Cares about their customers," "Good value for the money," and "Innovative." Normally, in a brand tracking study, there are usually between 30 to 40 statements. Typically they are divided into rational ("Good value for the money") and emotional ("Is a brand for me"). Respondents are often presented with a matrix of brands across the top and statements down the side. They must select the brands they believe match the statements on the left.

These statements are agonized over by the agency and the brand before launching the research. Usually, these statements are reviewed annually for relevance and interest. Some may be swapped out in favor of statements that better reflect a new advertising campaign or address a competitor's strategy. There is a lot of time and attention paid to these metrics. They think, "We have to get these right to be able to tell our clients what consumers think of their brand. It should be an exhaustive and thoughtful list." Often, that leads to long lists of 20 or more statements. What are respondents really answering at that point?

But we know that shoppers rarely think in these terms. Remember our question where you consider the last thing you bought? Where you were weighing purchasing between two brands? Did you think, "Well, this is a brand that cares about its customers, but the other one is trustworthy"? No. For the millionth time, *none of us think that way*.

What we think about is *our needs*. What problem is this purchase trying to solve, and which brand solves it better? Things we might be asking ourselves during the purchase process are:

- Will this dress make me feel confident at the party?
- Does this bread contain high-fructose corn syrup?
- Will this webcam make me look more professional for video meetings?

Notice something about those questions? The brand never comes into play there. Yes, brand matters, and it can be one of the deciding factors, but these questions are focused on solving *shoppers' problems*.

How Does My Brand Fare Against the Competitors?

One of the core benefits of brand tracking is the ability to define the competitive landscape. How do consumers view your brand, and are they more or less favorable towards you than they are towards your competitors?

Brand tracking is often done in a competitive context, starting with unaided brand awareness—What brands of [category] have you heard of? As always, the purchase funnel looms large here with every competitor's "funnel" categorized and compared to your brand's performance. In other words, the competitors get the same narcissistic treatment.

Ultimately, the competitive data is just as flawed. It is based on hypothetical perceptions of consumers. The data is focused on the brand, not the shopper. And, questions like personality and imagery statements bear little resemblance to the shopper's actual decision-making inputs. But there is even something more dangerous at play here. The competitive set is predetermined by the designer of the survey. That means as new brands and DTC channels emerge, the tracking study must adjust and increase in length to allow for the new addition. It also means the rise of those new brands will be ignored until it is too late. If a brand is not tracked initially, there is rarely a formal process to identify new competitors and include them in the research. By the time a new brand makes its way into the conversation, shoppers have already long been familiar with it.

Our Shopper Influence research does not define a competitive set. Rather, we explore the category as a whole. Let's illustrate this with a simple category like toothpaste. Traditionally, you would take a look at market share, identify the top competitors, and establish a competitive set for your tracking research. That set would then become static and any changes to it would impact all of the trending data.

Now, let's imagine a new toothpaste competitor comes along. A local organic favorite has just taken on national distribution. Their product is beloved and advocated for by their customers. All of their advertising has been through social media and their sales are direct to consumers. For more traditional brands, this upstart competitor could go unnoticed for some time. They aren't competing for your shelf space because they sell directly to the consumer. They aren't placing traditional media buys. All this results in the traditional brand having to learn about the competitor some time after they've made an impact large enough to get their attention. And maybe then it is too late and the market share is lost.

Our Shopper Influence work asks consumers what they purchased last. The competitive set is the actual brands being bought and as that upstart direct-to-consumer competitor started entering the scene, our client would know about it immediately. We'd also be able to track their growth in real time as their sales increased. Not only would we be able to track their growth, but we'd also understand why consumers were buying that brand, what sources of information they used to find that brand, what was most influential to them, how many defectors they were stealing from more established brands, and so on.

Essentially, brand tracking has a selection bias with a pre-approved competitive set. Shoppers do not operate within a limited set of brands. Our data showing the rise of Shopper Promiscuity proves this. Shopper Influence allows brands to change dynamically over time as they rise and fall in relevance according to the shoppers themselves.

Is My Marketing and Advertising Effective?

Brand tracking addresses advertising in a progressive series of questions intended to demonstrate the salience of the advertising. These questions mirror the Brand Narcissism that we have highlighted as problematic. The advertising questions typically follow the structure below:

- Unaided awareness: What brands have you seen advertising from in this category?
- Aided awareness: Have you seen any advertising for [BRAND]?
- Unaided recall: Have you seen this particular advertising? This question is then followed by an unbranded screenshot(s) of a video ad or an unbranded print advertisement.
- Unaided brand linkage: If yes to the above, what brand was this advertising promoting?
- Aided recall: Have you seen this advertising?

You can see the logic playing out here in terms of identifying how salient the advertising is to shoppers. If they recall seeing advertising for Diet Coke at the very first question, then we can safely assume the advertising has penetrated the shopper's subconscious. If a shopper cannot recognize the ad even after being shown the fully branded imagery, then they clearly have never been exposed to the advertising. There is a method at play here, but again, how much do these answers reflect the actual shopper experience with advertising?

There are a few key issues at play:

1 Brand tracking questions are asked among those intending to buy in the category. The assumption is that they are currently in the "research" phase and will be more open to receiving advertising messages. Our work

has shown, however, that a healthy percentage of shoppers can take less than a few minutes to go from undecided to decided in nearly every category. In fact, in automotive research, we've seen decision windows as short as three hours before purchase, despite the price tags that the category usually commands. This Intender classification will never capture those shoppers.

2   Intent does not guarantee action. Most brand trackers have long time frames in which a shopper can have the intention to buy. For the automotive category, the time frame can be as long as two years. Do you intend to buy a car in the next two years? Trackers are designed this way because tracking is expensive and broad intention time frames keep costs low. We understand the logistics of the decision to look at long purchase intention cycles, but most trackers are set so far out that, once again, we are asking respondents to think too hypothetically for their answers to be useful.

3   Brand tracking is often focused on measuring the media strategy that has the most dollars put behind it. This is because there is limited space in the questionnaire, so researchers have to focus on the media forms with the heaviest client investment. It is often the media that most brands and advertisers are focused on for that category at that time. However, our research has shown time and time again that shoppers are getting so much information from a wide variety of sources, most of which are not going to be addressed in tracking research.

4   This question structure really just measures how well respondents can recall the advertising. Maybe, among those who claimed to have seen it, there will be enough time to ask about some attributes. *Did it get your attention? Was the ad engaging?* But where in that question structure can we understand influence? How much did this advertising actually affect the outcome of a shopper's decision? Because the respondents are just Intenders, we cannot measure influence in a brand tracking study. Brands can't see which of their efforts actually made the difference.

By focusing on Recent Purchasers, we can solve all of these problems. Shopper Influence research captures:

• What sources of information were used? This includes all paid media, but also earned media, word of mouth, in-store and point of sale, and about fifty others.

• How influential was the source of information? Seeing an ad is only the first step in a long journey to making a difference in a shopper's thought process. Without influence, we lose any visibility into the *value* of that advertising.

- What content were you looking for from each source? People go to different media for different needs. Understanding how your shoppers are using media to gather information not only helps with messaging, but placement and spend as well.

- Who is buying my brand? Who is buying my competitors? With the DIAL (Defectors, Impulsives, Ambivalents, and Loyalists) we can identify not only who is buying your brand, but all the relationships shoppers have with your brand.

Ultimately, biased as we are, we think the outcome of this is very clear. Traditional brand tracking is not going to help a brand or advertiser make the right decision. Without the full scope of sources used, or without understanding influence or content, brands and advertisers are making guesses in the dark about what their shoppers need and when they need it.

How Have My Brand Metrics Changed Over Time?

One of the most powerful dynamics of brand tracking is the ability to see these metrics change over time. Brands love this because they can theoretically see their brand grow and evolve in almost real-time. Researchers love this because they get multi-year contracts with recurring revenue and a client that becomes dependent on the research they provide. Hopefully, this chapter has shown that the data coming out of brand tracking is not nearly as useful, accurate, or informative as it should be. Given the amount of money our industry takes in to do brand tracking, we should provide better results.

Trending data over time is very easy to do with Shopper Influence work. We simply run the research either continuously or in waves of research as traditional brand trackers do. This is the easiest question to answer for our clients. Additionally, one of the benefits of Shopper Influence is that we do not have to change the questionnaire to account for changes in the category. If new brands emerge, new purchase channels, or even disruptions that change the way the category operates, our questions remain the same. We can move with the category as it evolves rather than having to painfully adjust course on a legacy tracker and risk losing trendability. So, to that end, Shopper Influence research is actually more effective in trending analysis.

Brand tracking is not serving our clients, their brands, or their customers. The data emerging from it is flawed, often flat, and unable to generate actionable insights. Clients and researchers are often dissatisfied and frustrated with brand trackers, yet we keep running the same play. It is time to completely rethink this type of research from the ground up. When done correctly, brand tracking can be a vital, dynamic, and meaningful tool for researchers.

KEY TAKEAWAYS

- Brand tracking is rooted in the purchase funnel. Shopper Promiscuity has made the purchase funnel obsolete.

- Brand tracking is narcissistic. By focusing on the questions that brands want answered rather than how people are actually engaging with those brands, trackers yield poor data and unhelpful findings.

- Shopper Influence research solves these problems and still allows for trending over time, making it a superior research tool.

09

Unlocking Hidden Shopper Insights Through Agile Neuroscience

So far, we have focused our discussion on methods that use large sample sizes and stated data to reveal what drives shopper behavior. We know that asking a robust sample of shoppers about their recent behavior in a particular category yields good results. But it doesn't answer everything. Sometimes you'll hear marketers or skeptical stakeholders sneering at stated data and talking about how shoppers lie, either intentionally to present their best selves or unintentionally by omission. We wouldn't be in research if we didn't at some level trust shoppers to tell us what works and what doesn't, or what matters and what doesn't. We believe that you get good data if you ask good questions.

But there are some questions that shoppers can't answer easily. Not because they don't want to but because, as humans, we are not designed to be able to know what's happening in our subconscious. Evolutionarily-speaking, that's for a good reason. If we had to think about every single thing happening in our brain when we turn on a light switch or answer a text message, we would never be able to get anything done. According to neuroscientists, most of what the brain does—over 99 percent of it, by some estimates—is unconscious.

If the vast majority of the human brain's workings are unconscious, what impact does that have on researchers and marketers seeking to influence shopper behavior? Some readers may be familiar with neuroscience—maybe they have used it in their own research, or tried it on occasion. For others, this is totally new. We hope that this chapter will convince you that new and emerging tools are offering powerful ways to add dimension and depth to our understanding of the choices shoppers make. First, let's clarify what we mean when we talk about using neuroscience in market research.

Devora lives with a form of epilepsy and hates the idea of putting someone in an electroencephalogram (EEG) rig. When she was 10 years old, her neurologist used similar technology to induce a seizure to prove their diagnosis, and the experience was traumatizing. Traumatizing enough to make a 10-year-old think, "No one should ever have to go through this." Little did she know that she was going to become a researcher—and that one of the tools that she'd have to consider later in life would propose doing exactly that. But she knew from personal experience that putting anyone in an EEG was not a natural or pleasant experience—the exact opposite of the experience brands and retailers want their shoppers to have when interacting with their products or services.

Devora held to her belief and for years avoided proposing neuroscience-based research solutions that relied on having shoppers wear clunky, uncomfortable devices. We hesitated about using neuroscience in our research for other reasons, too. We wanted to be optimistic, but it just didn't feel reliable enough to offer up to clients because our experience seemed to indicate that the science wasn't fully proven and wasn't giving us or our clients a clear understanding of what was happening in the minds of shoppers.

Then, in 2018, Devora connected with a group that emerged from the Center for Neuroeconomics at Claremont Graduate University. Led by academic researchers Dr. Paul Zak and Dr. Jorge Barraza, their team had developed a neuroscience solution for market research based on 20 years of academic research. Engineered by a team of neuroscientists and cognitive psychologists and funded in part by the US Department of Defense's research and development agency, this new methodology is called Immersion. It didn't require the EEG caps that had traumatized Devora as a kid, and it was also distinct from the myriad other neuroscience solutions such as eye tracking or galvanic skin response (GSR) that had disappointed us in the past. What Immersion offered was an agile, scalable way to observe the signals that our hearts send. And, it turns out, by observing changing patterns of the heart, we can actually reveal what the brain loves. Immersion was the secret sauce we were looking for to complement our quantitative research efforts.

In 2020, in one of our last lunch meetings before Covid-19 shut down such banal things, Devora and our Managing Director Eddie Francis met with the Immersion team's co-founder Jorge Barraza and client partner Laura Beavin-Yates over yakitori in Downtown Los Angeles and hashed out the details of how we could collaborate. We'd partnered on some initial research studies and were convinced that the science was solid and that we wanted to go to market with their solution as a core tool in our research toolbox.

Laura Beavin-Yates, PhD, is our partner at Immersion, the plucky startup born from that CGU lab that has turned into a major force in neuroscience research. She explains the connection between emotional experiences and future action:

> Emotional experiences create memories. When we have emotional experiences, there's a physiologic thing that happens in the brain where we release these chemicals that actually tag those experiences as something meaningful and as something worth storing for later. It's something that drives decision making. It's something that ultimately guides whether or not someone continues to interact with your brand and chooses your brand repeatedly, gets onto your social media platform, engages with your content. We use emotion to tag meaning, because it helps to guide us through the world. It helps us know when we want to choose a certain product, when we are feeling great about going to a certain movie, who we want to spend our time with.

We tend to think about tagging content in the world of digital and social media—but it turns out that the brain tags information and experiences too. The brain tells itself to remember what signals are good, and what situations are not safe. It tags what's fun and engaging, and what's not cool. Our brains do this passively—without us even knowing it most of the time. Beavin-Yates suggests we think of the last movie we watched. Maybe it was yesterday, a couple of days ago, or a few weeks back. Whenever it was, we could ask respondents to think about that movie 30 minutes in. *How did you feel at the time? What were the emotions you were experiencing 30 minutes in? How about 45 minutes?* They would have a very challenging time answering those questions. They might be able to tell us which movie it was and be able to provide an overall assessment of its quality or entertainment value, but it would likely prove to be very challenging to really describe with accuracy what different scenes or content made them feel.

This, Beavin-Yates says, is difficult:

> A lot of the emotions that we experience on a day-to-day, minute-to-minute, or second-to-second basis are happening below the surface. If we had to constantly pause and think *What is my emotion right now?* we wouldn't be very functional when it comes to operating in the world. And so, a lot of those emotions that we experience throughout our day when we're navigating Amazon, selecting the right shampoo, or shopping for a new handbag we aren't even

consciously aware of, but our brain is constantly doing the work of tagging those experiences as emotional, as connected, as something that is of value or of meaning to us.

If you read Malcom Gladwell's *Blink* (2005), this concept will be familiar to you.

Because emotions are beneath the conscious surface, they are difficult to measure. At least, it used to be difficult to do so. Today, breakthroughs in neuroscience allow us to observe consumers and shoppers in their natural environments and passively track their emotions second by second as they are exposed to experiences or stimuli. Advancements and innovations in research and neuroscience are expanding our understanding of the human brain. We are now certain that these methods will continue to be an important part of the research we do to reveal what matters for shoppers and consumers.

Let's dig a little deeper with Immersion's Laura Beavin-Yates into how the science of tracking emotion works:

When the brain is having experiences and engaging with different things throughout the day, it is going through this automatic process where, again, it's saying, "Oh this is really fantastic. This is of value. I love this." As that happens, the brain and body release neurotransmitters and hormones that then cause a cascade effect throughout the body. When the brain is in a state of "immersion," which requires attention, but more importantly a high level of emotional connection, the brain releases oxytocin as a neurotransmitter, which actually binds in the brain, and the pituitary gland releases it as a hormone that binds to the vagus nerve. The vagus nerve extends from your brain stem down your neck, and then innervates your heart.

Our body has the largest concentration of oxytocin receptors in the vagus nerve, and when the oxytocin cascade occurs, the binding to the vagus nerve causes small changes in the way the heart beats. It's causing small shifts between the parasympathetic and sympathetic nervous systems. And we're actually able to capture those changes by passively tracking through fitness devices or smart watches. So, in essence, we use devices that people are wearing every day to already naturally track shifts in your heart rate second to second, and we're sending that data to the cloud in real time and applying our algorithms to look for distinct patterns that tell us when you're in this brain state of high immersion versus a state where you might be not finding as much value and are at risk of disengaging.

It wasn't always this easy, though—in fact, this work started with blood draws and hormone observation, and it took years of testing various methodologies to get to the current state where something as simple as a smartwatch can be used to know what's going on in the brain. As noted earlier, our friends at what is now Immersion started as the Center for Neuroeconomics Studies—an academic lab run by neuroscientist Paul Zak out of Claremont, California. In their early stages of work, the lab ran experiments where researchers would draw blood from subjects before and after engaging in different types of experiences to see how people's hormone levels were changing as a result, and then to evaluate how those hormone changes related to meaningful future behavior, like making a donation or a purchase.

Then Zak's team applied for and received a grant from the Defense Advanced Research Projects Agency (DARPA) and the US Department of Defense which challenged them to develop a methodology that was equally as reliable but could be used at scale and which could be validated by third party labs. DARPA was interested in a research method that could predict future behavior, but the organization needed it to be scalable and deployable on the battlefield. It wanted to know the answers to questions like—*If we drop a flyer to encourage people to put down their weapons, will it work?*

But jabbing people every ten minutes to see how their hormones are changing wasn't going to do the trick. The team was up against two challenges: their solution needed to be scalable and deployable in the real world—meaning no needles involved—and it needed to be validated by a set of third party academic labs. So Zak's team, which included Beavin-Yates and other researchers who still sit on the leadership team at Immersion, went to work and tested every neuroscience measuring technology they could find—256-electrode EEGs, breath analysis, medical-grade ECG devices, skin conductance, facial coding, even lasers. They also considered medical-grade devices that tracked heart rate and skin conductance. Beavin-Yates:

> We were looking for the strongest physiologic signal that correlated strongly with oxytocin release, but importantly, that it also served as an equally strong predictor of future decision making. And we found the most robust and predictive data stream was cardiac rhythm change— the small nuanced ways heart rate shifts second by second provides the strongest signal that people are in this brain state of immersion. Cardiac rhythm change was the most predictive data stream when it came to meaningful behavior—including data from other methodologies like galvanic skin response (GSR), EEG, facial coding which did not increase the predictive power at all.

In their early efforts, the team used medical-grade ECG devices to capture changes in cardiac rhythm change, widely known as heart rate variability (HRV). However, they knew that requiring chest placement of ECG electrodes did not truly meet the scalability challenge. To address this, they began exploring non-medical devices like fitness trackers, and eventually landed on an arm-based fitness tracker called a Scosche sensor. These devices proved to deliver data that tracked cardiac rhythm change as reliably as medical-grade devices were tracking HRV, and the team developed algorithms to ensure those signals provided an equally robust ability to predict meaningful behavior. It's essentially HRV 2.0.

When Covid-19 hit, the team decided to accelerate their efforts to allow for remote testing via smartwatches consumers already owned. Immersion identified a set of smartwatches that were reliable and developed device-specific algorithms to ensure all data would be comparable across devices.

Using consumer-owned smartwatches turned out to be a transformational opportunity for both our team and Immersion—not to mention because Covid-19 shut down most in-person lab testing indefinitely. Using smartwatches allowed us to scale neuroscience solutions for clients in ways that would have been previously impossible. As Beavin-Yates puts it:

> We don't have to bring people into a lab. We can find people who have smartwatches that already have these PPG sensors that track blood flow, and subsequently shifts in heart rate. They download an app, we measure their physiologic data and send it to the cloud for processing, and we output our measure of Immersion to the platform in near real-time. Immersion is a measure of attention— you need people to attend—but more importantly whether or not an experience is emotionally resonating. And it's on a simple scale from 1 to 100, with higher being better, higher being more likely to engage in some future behavior, and also peak moments corresponding with long-term memory.

For our team at Alter Agents, having a research tool that could complete our quantitative understanding of how to influence shopper behavior was a powerful moment. We'd always known there were limits to stated data—even when conducted among a large sample size and Recent Purchasers.

Zak says we have what he calls a Freudian hangover. He says:

> We somehow think from very poor reasoning by Freud that because the brain creates language, that if I just poke and prod hard enough I can get you to reveal the underlying reasons why you did something. But it's akin to asking your liver how it's processing your breakfast. You say that's just a silly thing,

but there's no way to make the unconscious data streams in the brain conscious. It just doesn't work that way. Hence, a measurement device is needed.

It gets even more difficult when we try to assess how much a respondent values something. Because, Zak says,

> Value is largely derived from emotional responses to a product or an experience. Those emotional responses, again, are largely out of conscious awareness. So, we say, rate how much you like this shopping experience, from one to seven. If we force people to give a number for the answer, the scientific question becomes, "*Does that number relate to anything useful?*"

This makes it challenging to get at how shoppers *feel* after they purchase. Remember, our quantitative data doesn't actually look for feelings. We just want to know what sources shoppers use and then how influential that source was on their purchase. But it gets much more complicated when a client asks us "How do they feel about their purchase?" Researchers will often add a couple of follow-up questions around satisfaction. But these questions always feel insufficient—we know that we have primed shoppers to give us the answers they want, because after making a purchase, how many will say "I hated this experience so much I bought this expensive jacket!"?

This is why stated data makes it difficult to determine what people will do in the future. However, when certain unconscious measures are met in the brain, it turns out that we can predict with about 80 percent accuracy what people will do in the future. We'll come back to using new tools to predict future action later in the chapter, but first let's take a look back at how far neuroscience has come since its early days, and why it's now finally at a place where researchers can apply it at scale to understand shopper behavior.

Neuroscience Back Then

Around 2002 neuroscience tools began to emerge in non-academic research settings. Before then, neuroscience was a tool only medical doctors or academic researchers could afford to experiment with. And, even then, few universities could support the cost of having functional magnetic resonance imaging (fMRI) and EEG technology readily available. The technologies required a lot of expertise, training, and cost to maintain and support. It could cost upwards of half a million dollars to run thirty people through an fMRI machine—that was something that simply could not be accessed by most marketers and brands. Furthermore, putting consumers into a claustrophobic metal tube isn't exactly what most of us would call a natural, real world experience (Levallois et al, 2021).

Scientists have long been aware that you can infer what's happening in the brain by measuring peripheral signals in the body (the scientific study of skin conductance began in 1900), but a breakthrough in neuroscience research came when experts realized that you could observe what's happening unconsciously by looking outside the brain at signals such as heart rate (Bell et al, 2018).

The realization that you don't have to listen directly to the brain to understand what the brain is doing helped to bridge the gap between academia and neuromarketing, and enabled the growth of neuroscience tools in market research. That was when early neuromarketing solutions like facial coding and eye tracking or GSR began to proliferate. These technologies provided researchers with new ways of understanding how consumers' brains were responding to stimuli, but they all came with significant limitations—most of all, they were rarely able to observe people in their natural environment. Here's a quick primer on the neuroscience tools sometimes used in market research.

Facial Coding

Facial coding was founded based on research conducted by Paul Ekman, who developed the theory that humans share seven universal emotional expressions: happiness, sadness, surprise, anger, fear, disgust, and contempt. Ekman's facial action coding system (FACS) trained researchers to code these expressions by watching for the activation of specific facial muscles (Lewis and Haviland-Jones, 2004). Today, when used for neuromarketing, facial coding uses consumers' webcams to record their facial reactions and then process these using algorithms tied to Ekman's seven universal emotional expressions. Facial coding results will typically reveal which emotions were present for most consumers during the experience. Although facial coding has been used widely because of its scalability and its promise to provide data on specific emotions, new research reveals our facial expressions don't necessarily capture much of our emotions, and they are not predictive of future action (Association for Psychological Science, 2019).

Eye Tracking

Eye tracking is a neuromarketing technique that is designed to measure consumer attention. The methodology uses cameras to track how a participant's eyes move when interacting with some stimulus like a website, an advertisement, or in-aisle experience. There are three primary kinds of eye tracking solutions: a computer-mounted eye tracking camera, face-mounted eye tracking glasses, and web-based eye tracking. Eye tracking is great for understanding where consumers are looking, when, and how long it takes to capture their attention.

Researchers began to rely on eye tracking with the idea that if someone is looking at something, it likely tells us they are attending to it. But the problem is that it doesn't tell us how engaged they are, or whether the experience they are attending to is actually working for them or not. For example, take a scenario where someone is standing in an aisle and they're looking at a lot of different things on the shelf, and it's taking a long time for them to make a decision. Are they having a hard time deciding because they are overwhelmed by too many choices? Or is it that they aren't seeing the pricing they're looking for? Unfortunately, eye tracking wouldn't reveal whether the experience was positive or negative. While eye tracking can tell you what is capturing attention, it doesn't illuminate the actual emotional impact or the value that a person is getting when having a particular experience during their shopping journey. It gives us some context, but it doesn't give the research team a deeper understanding of how the experience is connecting and whether or not this matters to a person.

Electroencephalogram (EEG)

EEG technology was designed to measure electrical activity in the brain during a particular experience. The kind of EEG that traumatized Devora may have had up to 256 electrodes that are placed on the head of the person being observed. For obvious reasons, EEGs are typically limited to a controlled lab environment. EEG devices are good at capturing activity accurately, but they don't necessarily identify where the activity is occurring, which makes it hard to understand the emotional impact of a particular experience. Emotion and memory centers are located deep within the brain, so when researchers record electrical activity on the top of the head, they can't actually tell if the activity originated in the outer cortex, or deeper brain areas.

This methodology also requires highly trained experts and weeks to process the data. Newer, lightweight EEG devices have been developed, but they have not proven to be effective in detecting emotional response to stimuli and experiences.

Galvanic Skin Response (GSR) / Skin Conductance (SC) / Electrodermal Activity (EDA)

GSR uses skin conductance, or electrodermal activity—that is to say, our sweat glands (found in our hands and feet)—to understand emotional arousal to a particular experience or piece of content. During testing, a GSR device will be placed on a consumer's finger, wrist, palm, or feet. While GSR provides fairly accurate readings of emotional arousal, it doesn't tell us if the arousal is positive or negative, because EDA shows similar increases when it comes to excitement, stress or anxiety. GSR also results in rather "noisy" data as it is susceptible to consumer movement and temperature changes, and must be completed in a controlled lab environment to be reliable.

Heart Rate Variability (HRV)

HRV captures the rhythm of the heart over time, which is effective in gauging emotional arousal. Medical-grade ECG devices are often used to capture HRV via electrodes that are placed on the upper torso of a consumer. Some solutions involve shining a light into the bloodstream and tracking the reflection of light to identify changes in the rhythms of the heart—also known as a photoplethysmograph or PPG sensor, which can be placed on the index finger or the ear. HRV data outputs in raw form and requires advanced expertise and significant time to process and analyze. This solution requires expensive equipment and can't be easily conducted in real-world settings.

Functional Magnetic Resonance Imaging (fMRI)

Many of us have experienced fMRI when we or a family member is being evaluated for a medical condition. Unfortunately, the technology is costly to deploy, and because of the need to put those being assessed into a large metal tube it is poorly suited for neuromarketing. fMRI uses magnets to measure changes in blood flow in the brain—it tells us which areas of the brain are active when exposed to different kinds of content. fMRI is good at detecting the general location of emotional activity, but because it picks up on blood moving to an area after it was active (the blood moves there to replenish resources), the time delay makes it hard to attribute changes to a specific element of an experience.

Agile Neuroscience and Completing Our View of the Shopper Journey

In contrast to many of the solutions described above, the Agile Neuroscience solution from Immersion that we use today allows us to capture the shopper or consumer experience second by second via smartwatches they already wear and are comfortable with. When we began using the technology as a component of our shopper research, we had a few requirements. We wanted the results to be accurate. We didn't want to have people shuffling around in EEG helmets. And we wanted to be able to collect the data in the environment where people were making decisions. And, finally, we wanted the neuroscience to be sound.

So the solution we landed on had to meet all these requirements. And, above all, it had to help us understand where shoppers lean in and where they make left turns—and then it had to be clear enough *why they did so.*

To understand how we can apply Agile Neuroscience to reveal what will connect with shoppers and how to optimize the shopping experience, let's look at what happens in the brain when we make decisions. Paul Zak reminds us that the first rule of thumb as it relates to brain behavior is that the "brain takes so much metabolic energy to run that it modulates that high energy overhead by trying to idle most of the time." Even making small decisions takes energy, so the brain is choosy about where it engages.

When it comes to shopping decisions, there are two core components that have to activate in a person's brain for them to decide to make a purchase:

1   A shopper has to orient themselves to that decision via the neurotransmitter dopamine, which acts as an orienting response. They have to think, *"This looks cool, there's something potentially useful or valuable to me."* According to Zak, "this is driven by the brain's core orientation system. It's deep in the midbrain, primarily driven by the neurotransmitter dopamine." In other words, the brain says, *"Ok fine, that looks interesting, I'll allocate resources there and pay attention."* As the brain starts focusing on the stimuli or experience, it continues to evaluate whether or not it's

getting a reward from that experience—if so, it will continue to pay attention.

2 The second part of the purchase decision is a "calculation." That is, according to Zak, "an evaluation the brain makes on the cost or difficulty of obtaining that thing that they've oriented to. This happens in a number of different areas in the brain but primarily in the temporal lobe, particularly in the area called the anterior insula. Consider when you bought your house and you wrote the check for the 20 percent down payment of that house cost, your palms were probably sweating." That, says Zak, is the insula giving us the bodily sensations that "*Hey, this is not a trivial purchase, there's risk here!*" And the bigger the cost, the bigger this activation is. When the brain starts to feel like there is less stress, and reduces the over-emphasis on the cost of this purchase, shoppers move closer to purchase. The key signal in the brain that "*I trust this person*," or "*I trust this experience*," is oxytocin. Oxytocin down-regulates that fear response to help us get over our inhibition; it tells us this product or service is sufficiently valuable and helps us ultimately say yes, even when risk is involved.

As a brand marketer, ideally what you want your ad or in-store experience to have consumer brains determine is that it is learning new things and experiencing something of value. Because when that happens, our brains start to release oxytocin. The oxytocin compels us to continue paying attention—and, more than that, our brains start to tag these experiences and store them for later.

Immersion's Laura Beavin-Yates puts it like this:

If a consumer is watching an advertisement that speaks to them in a way that they may not even be aware of, their brain will tag the experience as a way to say, "*Wait, this is meaningful. This is relevant. This is of value.*" The brain tags the information we are getting as worth saving for later, storing the experience to long-term memory. And then, when they are at the store and they are looking at the shelf, they may not even know or remember the mental tagging their brain did when they were getting value because they were immersed and much of this happens unconsciously. But the tagging that happened sends a signal to say, "*Hey, hey, look, this is that thing, remember?*"

So the brain works in the moment to keep us investing, but the work it does in that moment also guides our future behavior, so that we're more compelled to seek out that cool new car shopping site or purchase the perfume featured in the commercial featuring our favorite actor. A lot of times we're not even sure why we're driven toward that. It turns out it's because of the unconscious tagging of valuable experiences and the subsequent storage to long-term memory.

If the decision process to say yes to an experience or purchase were machine-like, decisions would be made in a very binary way. However, Zak points out that, as humans, these activities are distributed throughout the brain, which means if a shopper is tired or hungry they can get distracted or confused:

> If you think of the brain as a big cost–benefit calculator, then that cost–benefit is not objective, it's very much subjective. It is subjective based on how the experience is presented to me, my memories, my current physiologic state. So it means that there is not a single perfect shopping experience for everybody at all times.

This truth that "there is no single perfect shopping experience for everybody at all times" is the challenge of being a retailer or a brand that sells into retail. It's also the challenge of being a marketer who designs experiences and content for shoppers who may be in any state at any time. And, as researchers, it's something we are always trying to be mindful of.

Because shoppers can be in any state when we meet them, we meet them where they are, whether it be at home shopping on their phone, or browsing on their computer, or going to a store. We measure the whole journey—getting to the store and then going all the way through the store. We capture people in a natural environment and then understand that the results are actually going to apply to that environment because that's the environment they're going to shop in regularly. It's our belief that when you isolate things and put something in a white lab, you muddy the real-world impact of the results.

As we wrap up this chapter, let's look at how our team is applying these insights in real-world scenarios. Remember, our whole goal here is to understand the shopper experience and ultimately create better products and experiences for shoppers. We talked earlier about the role our Net Influence metric is playing to uncover influential moments and touchpoints during the shopper journey. Net Influence is stated, but Immersion and emerging neuroscience tools like it help complete our understanding of what drives decision making for shoppers.

To explore how you might apply this approach to improve the shopper or customer experience, here are a few key questions our clients have recently undertaken this research to address:

- Which media type is most immersive?
- What is the value of an engaged associate on the shopper experience?
- What is the impact of a new entertainment platform on the viewer experience?
- Which ad formats are most engaging?
- What kinds of creative best sell our products?
- What's the impact of AR on shopping experiences?
- What's the retail experience in our store like?
- What's the product experience of this new innovation like?

Research has revealed that higher immersion scores predict with about 80 percent accuracy what people will do in the future. So answering these questions for clients with confidence about their impact on future behavior is providing a powerful tool for brands to better influence shopper decision making. As Idil Cakim, SVP at Audacy, said of a recent study we partnered with her team on, "The neuro study we did together was as close to the truth as we could have gotten—there is no way we would've been able to measure that from just self-reports. It was phenomenal to get into biometrics and then translate them in actionable ways to business metrics."

Agile Neuroscience captures signals that are controlling the heart and the gut to map consumer and shopper attention signals combined with emotional resonance that are driven by dopamine and oxytocin. These signals would have remained unseen in a traditional quantitive or qualitative study—shoppers might not even remember having these experiences, or wouldn't think to self-report them.

We know, from our discussion on Brand Narcissism and Shopper Promiscuity, that the world is changing quickly. For brands to be adaptive and future proof their place in the market, they need to be open to new methodologies and thinking. Our Agile Neuroscience approach makes neurological research possible at scale and affordable. Layering this technique into other modalities of qualitative and quantitative research will create a full and vibrant set of insights.

KEY TAKEAWAYS

- Asking good questions isn't the only way to get solid insights. Sometimes there are key pieces of information that shoppers won't, or can't, tell us.

- Using a scientifically-proven neuro platform is important, but there are significant shortcomings inherent in some popular solutions that our industry has leveraged for several decades.

- A solution that's deployable at scale and can handle the real world can help us unlock truths about how shoppers feel in ways that we otherwise would be completely blind to.

References

Association for Psychological Science (2019) Weaknesses in emotion-expression research outlined in new report, Association for Psychological Science, July 17. www.psychologicalscience.org/news/releases/emotion-expressions-pspi.html (archived at https://perma.cc/UGD2-BFUQ)

Bell, L, Vogt, J, Willems, C and Routledge, T (2018) Beyond self-report: A review of physiological and neuroscientific methods to investigate consumer behavior, *Frontiers in Psychology*, 9, 1655

Gladwell, M (2005) *Blink: The power of thinking without thinking*, Little, Brown, New York

Levallois, C, Smidts, A and Wouters, P (2021) The emergence of neuromarketing investigated through online public communications (2002–2008), *Business History*, 63 (3), 443–66

Lewis, M and Haviland-Jones, J M (eds) (2004) *Handbook of Emotions*, Guilford Press, New York

10

The Evolution of Shopper Values

The world is built on stories. Brian Boyd, a university distinguished Professor of English at the University of Auckland, suggests that narrative was a key driver in our human evolution history (Boyd, 2017). Telling stories is quite literally built into our DNA. Paul B. Armstrong's work in *Stories and the Brain* talks about the interplay between neurology and narrative to illustrate how our brains rely on stories to organize all of the information we receive. This allows us to make sense of our world, to categorize what we are seeing, and to build meaning. Everything we do, everything we say, and everything we buy is built on a story that we tell ourselves.

As we discussed in our prior chapters, Brand Narcissism causes brands to assume their brand and their story is what really matters. They stop listening and start assuming. They don't actually do the work to see into the world of their shoppers. That singular "*What about me?*" focus makes brands blind to all the other things that matter to shoppers, including the stories shoppers tell themselves about what they buy and why.

It used to be that when you asked shoppers what matters most to them when making a purchase, they would almost always say, "*A good deal.*" And brand consideration was also often cited as a driver of purchase. However, in a lot of ways, these were default answers because shopper choices were far more limited than they are today. The brands shoppers saw at shelf were selected for them by retailers and distribution channels, and that was that. With limited choice, price was, by default, a key differentiator. When our options are limited, our stories, or our view of what is possible, is limited and less engaging. But that has changed in our unbound economy. Today we have nearly limitless options, so the stories we can tell have gotten far more interesting.

As anthropologist Michael Donovan wrote in his essay "The anthropology of shopping":

Good shopping, and successful retailers, provide the cues, symbols, and well crafted spaces that engage our cultural imagination. We can be an elegant consumer of couture (Neiman Marcus), a together family (Target), one of the boys (Best Buy), a capable homeowner (Home Depot), a playful courtesan (Victoria's Secret), an edgy iconoclastic egghead (The Mac Store), at least for a brief and breezy moment. We move in and out of retail's many living myths every day, assessing them, validating them, in a word, "living" them, and in the process making them ours. These are myths with a small "m"; not the Joseph Campbell variety, but myths all the same. That is, stories we tell ourselves about ourselves, about who we are, about who we could be, even if the artifice is very short lived.

Shoppers Do Research to Understand the Stories Products Tell

So it's no surprise that today, when we ask this question, the number one thing shoppers say they want before making a purchase is "*Information to feel confident about my decision.*" More than three in four say so.

Let's just stop for a moment and acknowledge that this single fact is a sea change in shopper values. Alongside the rise in Shopper Promiscuity and the parallel decline in the importance of brands, a whole new way of being has emerged for shoppers. They are now committed and adept researchers across all categories. They gather facts and figures, reviews and promotions, and their brains sort through them to give them confidence in their purchase decisions. Why are they so committed to research now?

As we've said, when shoppers enter a category, even one they may have bought from in the past, whatever product they are buying, be it electrolyte-infused water or premium coffee or a trip to Europe or a crib for their second child, they now enter the category with the expectation that there have been product improvements since they last purchased. They know things are constantly improving, because they are.

The pace of change is actually dizzying. Since the mid-1990s, there has been a 400 percent increase in the number of grocery SKUs (Ruhlman, 2017). According to the World Intellectual Property Organization, patent applications doubled in the last ten years to 3.3 million in 2018. And there were 119,928,851 products sold on Amazon in the US in April 2019 (ScrapeHero, 2019).

Today, shoppers can access nearly any product, nearly anywhere, at nearly any time. And as they do, their priorities are shifting. They are rethinking what matters to them and, with endless choice and constant innovation, they can afford to make meaning of the things they buy, and they expect the things they buy to have meaning. These factors converge to put incredible pressure on shoppers to be more informed, more aware, and more confident. With so much at stake, shoppers have become slightly (some of us very) neurotic—*Will I choose wisely? How do I know this is safe? What do the reviews say? What if I pick the wrong one? What if this product was made with child labor?*

When we talk to shoppers about what stops them from buying a product, there is an overarching sense of the "fear of the unknown." It's a factor that deters consumers from potential purchases or raises concerns. Our research finds that a majority of shoppers now scrutinize the ingredients and materials in the products they buy, and one in eight have concerns about the brand or company's credibility and reliability.

To help them sort through their questions, it's now a permanent habit to get others' opinions, with 62 percent of shoppers agreeing that user reviews are the most important pieces of input when making the final purchase decision, 56 percent using consumer reviews as sources of information for their purchases, and 33 percent using consumer reviews specifically to inform research about product quality and attributes.

Consumer reviews are now an integral part of nearly every consumer category. Whereas, in the past, the most important sources of information were seeing it in a store or a recommendation from a friend, today consumer reviews are one of the top sources of information. This is no accident. We want to hear other people's stories, too. Their stories help us organize our thoughts, create relevance to our own lives, and they connect us.

Shopping has typically been considered a highly transactional process. But shopping as it exists today is about much more than buying a product at a store. Shopping is an expression of who we are, who we want to be, and how we seek to live in the world. Shopping is a pastime, a kind of entertainment, and a validation of who we see ourselves to be—in other words, it's another story we tell ourselves. And when we can choose nearly anything to buy, the reason why we chose something matters. Even if it is just a story we tell ourselves. It is human nature to assign meaning, and when faced with limitless options meaning rises to become a critical part of the decision.

Donovan, the anthropologist, describes the central role that shopping plays in our culture today in his 2015 essay:

> Shopping is a central creative activity of American life, a kind of populist
> performance art. In shopping we connect with different facets of ourselves,

explore new ones, and enact any number of cultural ideals, myths really, about our social world. If you want a crash course in American attitudes about childhood, family life, masculinity, motherhood, class, and nation to name a few possibilities, go shopping.

So it isn't a surprise that the majority of shoppers acknowledge that the brands and products we buy represent our values and beliefs or other aspects of ourselves. Our research found that 64 percent of men and 60 percent of women say the products they buy are a reflection of their personality. Among ecommerce shoppers, this is even higher: 70 percent of those buying online say the products they buy are a reflection of their personality, as opposed to 48 percent of non-ecommerce shoppers. Younger shoppers are also more inclined to view their purchases as key to understanding who they are and what matters to them. The figure is 68 percent among Gen Z and Millennials, while just 43 percent of Boomers agree.

Pamela Marsh, PhD, heads up primary research at Omnicom Media Group. Her team has been studying the impact of Covid-19 on brand perceptions since 2020. She agrees that for Gen Z personal values play an important role in driving purchase decisions:

> There are brands with whom Gen Z would want to align or would not want to. A lot of that has to do with perception, as in they don't want to be perceived in a certain way. Or it's just truly in their heart that they wouldn't feel good about themselves purchasing from a brand that didn't do the right thing, or didn't care about their own employees, or didn't care about the environment. How you live, and who you are, and what you wear and what you buy, signals a lot of your identity for this generation. Young people are choosing to align with companies based on their purpose or their mission.

Shoppers Notice When the World Turns

And now, to further complicate things, the world is changing at a rapid pace. The climate emergency, environmental degradation, younger genera-tions' reinvigorated focus on social and racial justice, the recovery from a global pandemic and threat of those to come, the worldwide resurgence of authoritarian regimes, gender pay equity, growing wealth inequality, gov-ernmental and corporate corruption, war, migration, labor practices, invest-ment in local communities, sustainable farming, ethical sourcing of materials, the treatment of LGBTQ+ people, artificial intelligence, data privacy... We could go on and on about all of the issues and forces that are changing how we work and live.

Not surprisingly, when we talk to shoppers, Gen Z and Millennials are most concerned with these issues and it is impacting their buying decisions. But this isn't a momentary whim of an idealistic young person that could have felt this concern at any age, in any generation.

In the US alone, Gen Z has grown up alongside two decades of war, historically contentious presidential elections, the MeToo movement, Black Lives Matter, climate change, the election of the first Black president followed by a backlash that swept in one who stoked division and racial animus, and then a harrowing global pandemic which resulted in the deaths of over 840,000 Americans and 5.5 million deaths globally between the start of the pandemic and January 2022. So when we think about Gen Z, it's no surprise they are socially and politically aware—they have known nothing but instability and uncertainty.

Given this, Pamela Marsh underscores the way in which Gen Z has a different perspective from prior generations:

> Gen Z are acutely aware of politically correct and appropriateness and mission and authenticity and supporting things you care about. That did take off at different points in time with different generations but it's really powerful now. This generation are digital natives, they grew up with all kinds of new media... and so everything is amplified, and everything could be either supported or shunned in a second. And they have the tools, the power of communication... and they just can amplify their heart. They wear their hearts on their sleeves, whether that's done for altruistic reasons or *"Hello, I'm cool"* reasons.

Our point here is not political—it's that the clichéd yet apt phrase "corporate social responsibility" (CSR) is not a passing fad. The people in this social system have now become far more aware of what's happening in the world and what's at risk, so what they demand of not only their leaders but the brands they buy from has changed. We—and this is especially true for Gen Z and Millennials—have been trained to think about these things and be conscious about them. And these issues, which now form part of our stories, are the new norm.

So, what stories do shoppers find themselves aligning with? In other words, what causes do shoppers care about? And how much do they care?

New Stories, New Expectations, New Norms

As we have proven above, shoppers are now more knowledgeable than ever before. They are also living through a time when it seems like so many major issues are out of their control. Shoppers live in a chaotic world and can often feel that they are just along for the ride, unable to influence or alter the course of events. However, when it comes to their personal shopping decisions, they do have autonomy and power. They can vote with their dollars, they can make environmental decisions with their wallets, they can exert some pressure and influence through what they buy.

Our research finds further evidence that there is a global cultural shift from profit to purpose. And this shift is evident in shoppers' interest in myriad issues from organic products to labor practices to the B Corp revolution—a business model where a corporation decides to balance its mission and its bottom line by adhering to high standards of social responsibility, relationships with the community, charitable giving, diversity equity and inclusion, environmental impact, public transparency, and legal accountability. It has expanded significantly in a short time: there were over 3,000 certified B Corps at the start of 2020, compared to just 82 at the end of 2007 (Dixneuf, 2020).

As Jenifer Gorin, founder of the B Corp consulting company Impact Growth Partners told us, "a critical requirement for B Corp certification is the legal commitment which requires companies to take into consideration all stakeholders, not just shareholders, in decision making."

In the early 2000s, the corporate approach to this shift was shallow and came to be called "greenwashing." Clorox put out a green bottle and said it was environmentally friendly without even being remotely close, according to NBC News reports. Brands cloaked themselves in "greenness," but it was empty and meaningless. Shoppers caught on fast and began seeking out real brands that truly stood for the environmental cause, like Method, Honest Company, Whole Foods, and others.

We're well past those days. Today, brands know they cannot deceive shoppers and have to think about legitimately giving them what they are asking for. A 2019 study from Deloitte found that a majority of companies were increasing their commitments to sustainable business practices, with two-thirds saying that they were increasing their sourcing of renewable energy as a result of customer demands that they do so.

But it's not just about businesses being pushed by consumers—there are other reasons for them to become more sustainable. Gorin adds: "Companies that have been thoughtful about their supply chains (as required by B Corp certification) may screen their suppliers, demand industry-specific certifications, or prioritize local suppliers and are therefore more likely to have better outcomes in challenging environments."

Indeed, after the pandemic laid bare some of the inefficiencies and weaknesses of the global supply chain, businesses looked to sustainability as a key part of resilience. They had somewhat of a game plan to fall back on, as some were already looking to source raw materials more locally in order to cut transportation costs and emissions, recycled more material, and even invested in more AI-enabled technologies to hunt down inefficiencies (Raw, 2019). That also bore out in the markets, where funds with ESG criteria outperformed the standard indices as investors viewed sustainability as a strength in hard times, not a burden (Feuer, 2021).

Gorin notes:

Stakeholders, in particular customers, suppliers, and employees, are seeking meaningful social and environmental action, and transparency around companies' impact. Businesses are responding because they see that taking substantial action and being transparent support their business case.

That business case could not be more clear for an increasing number of shoppers. Shoppers and consumers now *expect* brands not only to behave well but also to be proactive in their commitments. This comes through protecting their data (59 percent), maintaining consumer satisfaction standards (57 percent), and treating employees well (53 percent).

Environmental and sustainability concerns are the next most important factors shoppers take into consideration when making purchasing decisions. Previously, our research found that between 15 and 25 percent of shoppers had concerns related to environmental practices, but that has grown significantly over the past decade. Today, 54 percent of shoppers care about the impact a product has on the environment. When we look at those who spend liberally, that figure rises to 63 percent. About half of shoppers who are more cost-conscious agree. Meanwhile, 44 percent of shoppers report considering a brand's environmental responsibility before they purchase.

Shoppers also now expect greater transparency from brands about their business practices, with 43 percent saying this is a consideration prior to purchasing. And over a third of shoppers say they want to be in-the-know about a company's manufacturing practices. However, this really depends on how eco-conscious a shopper is. Forty-three percent of eco-conscious shoppers agree, while just 29 percent of their less eco-conscious counterparts do.

When we ask about their expectations of brands, non-white shoppers care more about specific social and environmental issues, which may stem from a more personal stake at play (Table 10.1).

TABLE 10.1   Share of shoppers saying that an issue is important to them, by majority and non-majority racial groups in the United States

	White	Non-white
Making a positive difference in the world in which we live	44.0%	49.2% ↑
Equality (e.g. gender, race, sexuality, etc.)	42.4%	50.1% ↑
Innovative/forward thinking	41.5%	45.5% ↑

The Impacts of Economic Power and Generational Attitudes

However, while shoppers across ethnicities are expressing increasing concern and interest in brand social responsibility, it's also true that white economic privilege allows more room for these worries. Lower income groups are less likely to have the liberty to take into consideration brands' stances on social, economic, and environmental justice issues.

When we look at shoppers from households earning above and below $60,000 in annual income, we see on average an eleven point difference between these cohorts on issues including being environmentally responsible (48 percent vs 39 percent), organic/non-GMO farming (43 percent vs 29 percent), giving back to charity (43 percent vs 34 percent), and providing affordable healthcare to their employees (44 percent vs 35 percent) (Table 10.2).

Economic power does allow shoppers to ask more of brands, and those with that power are doing so. However, an interesting finding from our data shows that Covid-impacted shoppers (those whose shopping habits were meaningfully or significantly changed due to Covid-19) tend to care more about *all* causes compared to those not as directly impacted by Covid (Table 10.3). From treating employees well (58 percent vs 41 percent) to making a positive difference in the world (50 percent vs 32 percent) to equality (49 percent vs 32 percent) Covid-19 appears to have made a mark on shoppers

TABLE 10.2   Share of shoppers saying that an issue is important to them, by annual household income bracket

	< $60,000 annual household income	$60,000+ annual household income
Environmentally responsible	39%	48% ↑
Organic/Non-GMO farming	29%	43% ↑
Giving back to charity	34%	43% ↑
Providing affordable healthcare to employees	35%	44% ↑

who were impacted by the virus and has caused them to think differently about their expectations of brands. This doesn't just play out in our market research. Psychology researchers from the University of California—Los Angeles and Harvard University found that the pandemic spurred those in the US to think more about supporting one another and being more community-focused. They also posit that this frame of mind may have helped feed the mass participation in the Black Lives Matter protests that came about during the pandemic as well (UCLA Health, 2021).

TABLE 10.3   Share of shoppers saying that an issue is important to them, by Covid-19 impact status

	Covid-impacted shoppers	Non-impacted shoppers
Treating employees well	58% ↑	41%
Making a positive difference in the world	50% ↑	32%
Equality (e.g., gender, sexual orientation, race, etc.)/ Equal justice	49% ↑	32%

Generational differences also play a huge role in determining how shoppers view their buying power in social terms. Our data shows a consistent trend: younger generations are more likely to tie a brand or company's real-world impact on society to their shopping decisions.

When we look at product and manufacturing practices in particular, we start to see greater daylight between younger and older shoppers, with

57 percent of Gen Z and Millennials saying they care about a product's impact on the environment, compared to 45 percent of Boomers. Moreover, 42 percent of Gen Z and Millennials will go out of their way to know more about a company's manufacturing practices, while only 21 percent of Boomers say they will do so.

Table 10.4 depicts generational differences in CSR-related company policies and practices that shoppers evaluate to be a deal breaker or strong consideration when making purchases from specific brands. Gen Z, Millennials, and Gen X shoppers tend to be significantly more cognizant of and exhibit a deeper care for considering these factors than their Boomer counterparts.

TABLE 10.4   Share of shoppers saying that an issue is important to them, by generation

	Gen Z/ Millennials	Gen X	Boomers
Treating their employees well	55.1%	53.2%	44.6%
Supporting the local economy	48.7%	50.3%	43.5%
Making a positive difference in the world in which we live	48.0%	45.4%	33.0%
Equality (e.g., gender, sexual orientation, race, etc.)	48.0%	43.0%	31.4%
Environmentally responsible	47.1%	44.3%	34.8%
Innovative/forward thinking	45.2%	43.1%	30.6%
Transparent business practices	44.4%	44.2%	37.8%
Providing affordable healthcare to their employees	43.1%	41.1%	27.3%
Giving back to charity	41.5%	38.8%	29.9%
Organic/non-GMO farming	38.4%	37.8%	25.3%

Furthermore, the generational gaps broaden when looking at identification with the shopping attitudes in Table 10.5 concerning brands' alignment with ethical and sustainable practices. Concurrent with the transgenerational cultural shifts from profit to purpose, Gen Z and Millennials show a much stronger identification than Gen X shoppers, and an even greater divergence from Boomers.

TABLE 10.5   Share of shoppers agreeing with the statement, by generation

	Gen Z/ Millennials	Gen X	Boomers
I care about the impact a product has on the environment	57%	52%	45%
I need to know as much as I can about the manufacturing practices of the brands I buy	42%	35%	21%
I always buy products that are all natural or organic	58%	53%	38%

Pamela Marsh advises us that these numbers speak to Gen Z's awareness and power:

> Gen Z is a very aware generation. They are a very involved generation, politically, environmentally, ethically speaking about a lot of causes, a lot of issues. They do expect the brands who they want to align with and buy, and purchase from, to align with their beliefs, their mission, their points of view, and I think that they don't also have the longevity that older generations have. They're not as tried and true with brands, just purely based on age. Older generations who grew up with brands and who have stuck with brands want to give them a second chance if they've done wrong. Gen Z have a lot of power, possibly unprecedented power, that they wield over brands, but also over other generations... of what brands to purchase across an array of categories.

Given these trends and shifting values, let's return to where this chapter began: stories. The stories brands create and tell must undergo a radical transformation to meet increasingly promiscuous and demanding shoppers where they are at. And lip service won't cut it. Matt Stefl, Clinical Professor of Marketing and Co-Director of the M-School at Loyola Marymount University, put it succinctly when he said that "Brands need to act, not say. Don't tell me you're dope. Just be dope." So if it's going to be real and it's going to resonate with shoppers, brands will have to dig deep to understand how to behave in this new world. And that's got to start with the questions their research is asking.

KEY TAKEAWAYS

- The number of choices that shoppers have has led them to begin thinking about what the product they choose to buy says about them.

- Younger generations and those with a higher household income are more likely to connect their purchase decisions with global trends and causes.

- Successful brands have caught on to this and are taking action to align with the values of the growing parts of their customer base.

References

Armstrong, P B (2020) *Stories and the Brain: The neuroscience of narrative*, Johns Hopkins University Press, Baltimore

Boyd, B (2017) The evolution of stories: From mimesis to language, from fact to fiction, *Wiley Interdisciplinary Reviews: Cognitive science*, 9 (1), 1444

Deloitte Insights (2019) *Deloitte Resources 2019 Study—Energy Management: Balancing climate, cost, and choice.* www2.deloitte.com/content/dam/insights/us/articles/5065_Global-resources-study/DI_Global-resources-study.pdf (archived at https://perma.cc/4GDZ-VY6D)

Dixneuf, S (2020) B Corp: People, environment and profits, Suston Magazine, February 7. https://sustonmagazine.com/2020/02/07/the-rise-of-b-corps/ (archived at https://perma.cc/7ZGX-L76R)

Donovan, M (2015) The anthropology of shopping, Practica Group. https://practicagroup.com/assets/uploads/2015/11/Anthropology_of_Shopping.pdf (archived at https://perma.cc/3SR5-GVZ5)

Feuer, W (2021) Here's more evidence that ESG funds outperformed during the pandemic, Institutional Investor, April 7. www.institutionalinvestor.com/article/b1r9gb5p9k10b4/Here-s-More-Evidence-That-ESG-Funds-Outperformed-During-the-Pandemic (archived at https://perma.cc/AXP2-XG8E)

Raw, E (2019) 3 sustainable manufacturing trends for 2020 and beyond, Reliable Plant. www.reliableplant.com/Read/31850/sustainable-manufacturing (archived at https://perma.cc/D6N7-TQEN)

Ruhlman, M (2017) *Grocery: The buying and selling of food in America*, Abrams, New York

ScrapeHero (2019) How many products does Amazon sell?—April 2019. www.scrapehero.com/number-of-products-on-amazon-april-2019/ (archived at https://perma.cc/MMT4-LSFN)

Tennery, A (2009) The four biggest "green" marketing scams, NBC News, 22 April. www.nbcnews.com/id/wbna30334853 (archived at https://perma.cc/2LXZ-RSLF)

UCLA Health (2021) Internet trends suggest Covid-19 spurred a return to earlier values and activities, 18 February. www.uclahealth.org/news/internet-trends-suggest-covid19-spurred-a-return-to-earlier-values-and-activities (archived at https://perma.cc/E2EQ-YKQG)

11

The Covid Inflection Point

The arrival of Covid-19 changed everything. Every non-fiction book written in the next fifty years, at least, will address how Covid-19 impacted their book's topic. We do not even know yet the extent to which the virus will reshape the world. Today, in 2022, we are still discussing death and infection tallies, vaccination rates, and economic challenges. The longer-term impact on economic forces, public health policies, political parties, and our society's trajectory is yet to be discovered. Twenty years into the future, we'll be referring to our children and grandchildren as the "Covid generation" and the psychological, economic, and social impacts the virus imposed on them. We know this because research has proven that widespread social trauma takes decades to heal.

Think about the Great Depression and the trauma it caused. That economic calamity left scars on the psyches of entire countries around the world and helped push us into a global conflict that killed upwards of 75 million people within two decades of Black Tuesday. Rebecca's grandparents were raised in Portugal during that period of backbreaking hardship. Her family left those bleak economic prospects and came to the United States, prospered, and quickly moved up into the working middle class. That was 80 years ago, but Rebecca's family still tells stories about Grandpa Tony bringing home his brown paper lunch bag, stained and wrinkled, to be used again the next day. That commitment to frugality, born from serious hardship, stuck with him. He never forgot the lessons and values he learned in his youth that shaped so many decisions and behaviors in his life. And his experience with the Depression was widely shared with his entire generation—growing up in hard economic times impacts people's economic decisions for decades to come. The same will be true for all of us regarding the pandemic, and it will be especially true for the young generation growing up in a world where they will only have faint memories of life before Covid-19 turned it all upside down. Covid will still matter in 2080, and people doing our jobs in the market research industry will be able to point to specific human behavior and correctly infer that Covid made it happen.

The pandemic has shown us how many of our society's systems were fragile or already broken. We had been holding things together, in some cases barely holding it together, and the pandemic has shined a bright light on some of the harsh realities of our existence. Schools and childcare shutdowns quickly exposed how fragile the childcare ecosystem is in the United States. Families had cobbled together resources and support networks only to see them suddenly pulled away with no replacement. Our healthcare system quickly buckled under the weight of enormous demands for personal protective equipment, oxygen, ventilators, and staff. We had to redefine what made a worker "essential," realizing that we needed grocery shelf stockers as much as we needed nurses, despite the gulf in perceived social value between those professions. And the polarization in the American political system that had already begun shredding the edges of truth bred a strain of vaccine hesitancy that led to the needless suffering and deaths of thousands. This is widespread social trauma.

In March and April of 2020, we heard a common refrain that this pandemic would be the "great equalizer" and that "*We are all in this together.*" That well-meaning intent was abandoned when we started to see the huge disparity of the virus's impact. Upper middle-class knowledge workers could move their work into their homes and continue drawing paychecks. But those in low-income jobs were sent home without any financial recourse, losing hourly wages that they needed. The racial disparities in access to healthcare services were revealed plainly for all to see, with our data finding that Black and Hispanic Americans were more likely than their white counterparts to have known someone who was sickened or killed by the virus (Alter Agents, 2021). The transfer of wealth to millionaires and billionaires pulled resources from those who were already teetering on the edge of financial instability. Despite an eviction moratorium throughout 2020 and most of 2021, urban streets seemed to flood with homeless people, while housing prices pushed even higher. There was never anything *equal* about this pandemic.

Just before this all started, Alter Agents had embarked on a three-part study titled Facing Fear, which studied how scared and uncertain Americans were feeling. We gathered data for the first wave in November of 2019, unaware that a global disaster was looming around the corner. Two more waves of research over the subsequent twelve months laid out in stark detail

FIGURE 11.1   Share of US ethnic groups affected by Covid-19

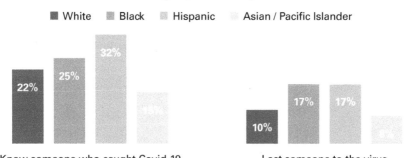

the psychological impact this was having on the American consumer. Peter Atwater, an economist and Professor at the College of William and Mary in Virginia, spoke with us about the K-shaped recovery he saw coming our way. In economics modeling, recessions and recoveries can be charted as a line graph, where that line represents GDP or another measure of activity. In a normal, short recovery and recession, the line is shaped like a V, where the sharp downward slope represents the country's economic health declining, followed by a sharp upward slope that measures the rebound. However, in a K-shaped recovery, only a portion of the population recovers like the V graph shows, making up the upper arm of the "K." The other half of the population either keeps losing altitude or limps along at a shallower incline, forming the lower arm of the "K." The arm and the leg just keep getting farther and farther apart as time goes on. It's a permanent state of widening inequality, absent concerted intervention.

That is exactly what we've seen come to pass. The topline numbers in mid-2021 looked good: GDP bounced back, the stock market recovered, and unemployment has been trending downward for over a year. Yet the recovery is very uneven. A report from financial giant Capital One found that even in August of 2021, sixteen months after US GDP began to rebound from the technically short Covid recession, the recovery was significantly slower for lower-wage workers, who even reported feeling less secure in their jobs then than they did at the start of the crisis. Higher-income households are in a much better position relative to lower-income households because they had the means to better weather the storm (Capital One Insights Center, 2021).

The K-shaped recovery is not only economic. According to Atwater, the cause of the K-shape is, "at its core, not an economic issue. It's a sentiment issue, a confidence issue, an issue of vulnerability."

FIGURE 11.2   Percentage of US economic groups expressing optimism in their future

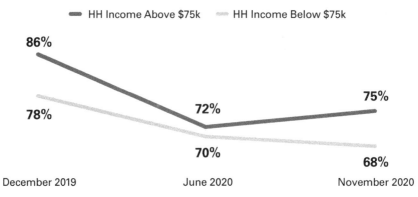

Our Facing Fear research also looked at the psychological impact of Covid and the economy. The "K" shape was apparent in the trended data from Facing Fear, which ran to December of 2020. Those graphs, where we split respondents roughly along the median US household income, were so stark and obvious that it took us aback. For Americans above the average household income, we saw a rebound of positive statements like "*I think my future will be better.*" We saw evidence of optimism returning to this group, while Americans in households with below-average incomes continued to drop on these metrics (Figure 11.2).

Atwater spoke to us at the time about the emotional impact of recessions, framing the idea around high confidence and low confidence. The economic K also creates a confidence K, as people with greater economic means feel more secure about their place in the world, while those with lower incomes carry the burden of increasing anxiety and fear. This creates a scenario where the CEOs, financiers, and policy makers are pushing for growth and investment while their workers continue to feel left behind, reading topline profit numbers for their employers that are absolutely alien to their daily life. The rise of strikes, union engagement, and demand from workers for higher salaries illustrates how different the conversation is among these two groups. The tension, driven by economics and mindset, will continue to divide us until we start pulling towards a common goal of greater general prosperity. The economic vulnerability felt by those on the leg of the "K" leaves them in a constant state of heightened alert. "It's incredibly exhausting," Atwater says, and pushes people to focus on immediate problems: what he calls the "me, here, now" mindset.

Let's stop here and take a breath. This is tough stuff to talk about and we certainly don't have the expertise, time, or resources to address all of these issues to the degree they deserve in this book. But it is important to understand the broad context for how all of the above, that collision of long-term trends and global calamity, is affecting shoppers. This same economic and emotional confidence divide between people in our society also shapes how they shop. Brand managers, advertisers, and researchers need to understand that, and look for how it is affecting their customers and audiences.

In an earlier chapter, we talked about the expectation of innovation. With so much rapid change in the past ten years, shoppers are now asking themselves, "*What's new?*" every single time they decide they need to buy something. After the broad impact left by Covid, they are also regularly asking themselves, "*Why does it have to be this way?*" We have been re-evaluating our lives, our social systems, and our approach to work. It makes sense that shoppers are also re-evaluating their expectations and experiences when they shop.

Covid's Impact on Shoppers

"I don't believe that we get through this in a tidy way that has this 'Roaring 20s' environment when we're all done," says Atwater. "We've got a period of societal resolution to get through first."

An aspect of the Shopper Influence research that we've been discussing throughout this book looked at the way that shoppers have been impacted by Covid. The findings surprised us and highlighted the powerful ways in which the K-shaped recovery impacts more than just economics. Before we get into the data, let's discuss how we are segmenting the population based on Covid impact. Our approach was to look at the way Covid had impacted our respondents' working situations. We learned through our Facing Fear research that job insecurity plays a huge role in how people behave. So, we decided to look at the impact of Covid through that lens. We divided our respondents into three groups: those whose employment location and hours were unchanged, those who lost their jobs because of Covid, and those who were able to work remotely (Figure 11.3).

Our research shows that those who have begun working remotely due to Covid have dramatically altered their shopping habits, so we're going to really dive into their answers. They behave quite differently from the other two groups. We'll get into the details of what this looks like below, but let's

FIGURE 11.3   Percentage of Shopper Influence respondents affected by the pandemic to differing degrees

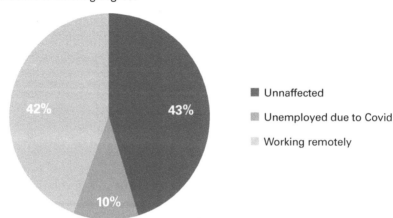

first dissect why this might be. As we've seen with the K-shaped recovery, there is a portion of the population that will suffer less economic and emotional damage, and will rebound faster. That is exactly the case with the remote workers in our Shopper Influence study. Starting with the demographics, we see that our remote workers very much reflect higher-income workers, with advanced educational degrees and more disposable income.

Remote workers are more likely to:

- be white (83 percent)
- be married (64 percent)
- be high earners (42 percent reported over $100k in annual household income)
- have children in the home (69 percent)
- have a four-year college degree or advanced degree (65 percent)

This group enjoys several advantages over the rest of the population. They are less likely to be impacted by socioeconomic factors that disadvantage minorities. They are more likely to be in dual-income households. They are more likely to have specialized skills that protect their employment status. Plus, they began this pandemic likely to be more financially stable than others in the first place.

All of these factors lead to a unique and privileged professional working class that has not only been able to weather the impacts of Covid, but position itself to take advantage of circumstances to even improve upon their position. This bit of research points to the broader trend wherein those with existing advantages gain opportunities, while the disadvantaged continue to feel more pain and watch their challenges increase as inequality widens.

Time is a Luxury for Remote Workers

Time is a luxury, and we see that play out in how our respondents behave. Those who are working remotely are taking more time to make purchase decisions, with significantly fewer of them making purchase decisions within the same day (Figure 11.4). These are the people leaving items in their digital carts for days while they research other options, to the chagrin of ecommerce managers. One of the huge benefits of working remotely is that you can shop at your relative convenience. Online shopping is clearly easier to do when you're at your computer all day without the possibility of a coworker seeing what you're doing on company time. Even in-person shopping is more convenient, as remote workers can pop out for a few moments between meetings or at lunchtime. Remote work allows people more flexibility in life, and that influences their shopping behavior.

FIGURE 11.4   Percentage of Shopper Influence respondents in each Covid-19-impacted employment group spending one day or less on their purchase decision

More Time Means More Research

With the flexibility brought by being in control over more of their time, remote workers also have the opportunity to do more research before making a purchase decision. We found that remote workers are using 50 percent more sources than others when they make a purchase. That data cuts across all product and service categories we researched in this study. From dog supplements and treats to home furnishings, remote workers are taking advantage of the time they have to do more research on their shopping (Figure 11.5).

The takeaway from this data is that shoppers will do more research *if they can*. Time, the immediacy of needs, and other factors might actually be deflating the number of sources shoppers would use if only they had the time.

FIGURE 11.5   Average number of sources used by people in each Covid-19-impacted employment group

Tying back into our discussion about Shopper Promiscuity, remote workers are also much more likely to use search engines than the other groups (Figure 11.6). This tells us that remote workers are starting more from a 'clean slate' perspective rather than thinking about retailers (online or otherwise) or a brand. Imagine a scenario where a remote worker needs to buy a new vacuum. We know that they expect there to have been innovation in that category since the last time they purchased. They also likely expect there to be new brands and maybe even new distribution channels that they will want to explore. So, starting with a broad search gives them an overview of the category and options for where to dive deeper for further information. Now, imagine the same need, a vacuum cleaner, for someone who is still working in a physical workplace. They have fewer hours in the day to devote to their shopping process. They don't have the luxury of starting from a broad view. They need the vacuum cleaner more quickly and they are going to be efficient in how they go about getting it. Same with someone who is unemployed. While they may have more time, they are likely very financially cash-strapped. Their expediency is probably due to pre-limiting their activity to vacuum cleaners that fit their budget.

FIGURE 11.6   Percentage of Shopper Influence respondents in each Covid-19-impacted employment group using search engines in their purchase decision

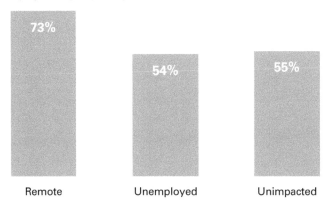

Remote   Unemployed   Unimpacted

Another interesting impact of working outside an assigned office is that doing so allows shoppers to spend more time seeking out the best price. Remote workers are significantly more likely to use price-related sources than both those who lost their jobs due to Covid and those that were not impacted at all. When you have the luxury of time and the ability to look at a variety of options, you can hunt for the best deals. You also have the time to sign up for coupons and offers, download apps that scan for discounts, and spend time reviewing those sources for offers that work for you. It would be natural to assume that unemployed people would be the leading group on price-related sources, but we know that they are often not able to take advantage of sales in the way that people with higher incomes are.

This is due to the inequality that's baked into most purchases. Think about buying laundry detergent. The bulk detergents are sold at an overall lower price per unit than the lesser-quantity options. Buying in bulk is an advantage for the consumer because it lets their money work harder. But if you have a very limited budget and only $7 to spend on laundry detergent during a given shopping trip, you will be forced to buy the smaller amount that costs more per unit. This dynamic plays out in a lot of other ways. Online offers that provide free shipping often require a minimum purchase amount for that benefit to kick in. There are also lots of great discounts if you can buy something full price first or spend a minimum of $50. All of these offers are great for many consumers, but only if they have the money to buy their way into taking advantage of them in the first place. What results is a situation where those above a certain income threshold save money in the long run and get richer, while those with incomes below that threshold are unable to save as much money and become relatively poorer.

That cycle self-reinforces the longer it goes on, building a group of permanently price-sensitive shoppers.

FIGURE 11.7   Percentage of Shopper Influence respondents in each Covid-19-impacted employment group using coupons or promotional discount apps during their purchase journey

Time Leads to Increased Defection

In an earlier chapter, we showed you the Shopper DIAL—made of Defectors, Impulsives, Ambivalents, and Loyalists. This chapter has already revealed that remote workers are significantly less impulsive than the other two groups. But, fascinatingly, they are more likely to defect from the brand they had in mind.

FIGURE 11.8   Percentage of Shopper Influence respondents in each Covid-19-impacted employment group agreeing with the statement "I did additional research into the brand and didn't like what I learned"

For brands, a clear problem with a more informed and well-researched public is the higher risk that they may learn something that turns them away from your brand. Not only does this happen more frequently among remote workers, but it happens at nearly double the rate of those not impacted by

Covid and at *five times* the rate of those who are unemployed. Ultimately, what this tells us is that remote workers are a more discerning group and also more sensitive to purchase barriers or negative experiences they encounter during the shopping process.

When time is on your side and you have access to multiple resources, abandoning a brand that just doesn't feel right is a much less risky option to take. If you have qualms, you can absolutely keep shopping. Those who are unemployed have less financial freedom to be so selective. And those who are still working on-site have less time to be so discerning. Remote workers are an attractive target market—they spend more because they tend to have more disposable income. But they have become a riskier group to rely on during Covid because they are harder to court. They are more willing to wait to buy, they are more likely to defect to another brand, and they are using their time to be more informed about every purchase.

Time Generates More Barriers

We see another aspect of this play out when it comes to the challenges or obstacles shoppers face during their shopper journey. Again, with the luxury of time comes increased discernment and sensitivity. It was the remote workers we surveyed who encountered the most obstacles when shopping (Figure 11.9). It naturally follows that doing more research and spending more time on decision-making would expose a shopper to an increased number of barriers. When you add in the fact that one in four shoppers who started with a brand in mind found something they did not like during their research process, you can see the huge impact this extra research is having on remote workers' behavior.

FIGURE 11.9   Percentage of Shopper Influence respondents in each Covid-19-impacted employment group reporting that they encountered barriers to purchase during their shopping journey

Barriers are also more heavily encountered by those who are unemployed, with significantly more of them hitting the obstacle of "It was too expensive" (Figure 11.10). Again, this follows logically that this group would have more financial challenges and be more sensitive to price.

FIGURE 11.10   Percentage of Shopper Influence respondents in each Covid-19-impacted employment group reporting that they encountered the barrier "It was too expensive" during their shopping journey

Shoppers Who Spend More Time are More Likely to Share Their Experiences

One aspect of our Shopper Influence research that we did not discuss at length in our earlier chapters is Refraction. We use the term "Refraction" to classify what shoppers did, if anything, after purchasing the item in terms of sharing that experience. We offer up multiple possible ways to share, from speaking with friends and family or posting on social media to writing a review or recording a video. In this sense, we once again see remote workers behaving differently than their peers (Table 11.1). We know from the research that remote workers are more informed, researched, and challenging to please. But a silver lining on this group of persnickety customers is that they are significantly more likely to share their experience with others.

This makes perfect sense and there are several factors leading to an increase in Refraction. We know remote workers do a lot more research. They also take longer from entering a category as a shopper to making a final purchase decision. They encounter more barriers and one in four of them abandon the brand they originally had in mind. Overall, these factors come together to create a much more complex and engaging "story" than a harried on-site worker might by swinging by the grocery store to pick up

TABLE 11.1   Shopper Influence respondents in each Covid-19-impacted employment group reporting that they shared information about their recent purchase experience

83%	Remote workers who shared information about their experience on an average of 3 different channels
72%	Unemployed workers who shared information about their experience on an average of 2 different channels
61%	Unimpacted workers who shared information about their experience on an average of 2.6 different channels

something pre-made to pop in the oven for dinner. Remote workers have more to talk about and spend more time becoming invested in the purchase.

High Refraction also makes these shoppers more valuable to brands. A good interaction with a brand, the product, and the experience of shopping for it are all wonderful stories that can advocate for a brand. It's like the positive earned media we all so crave. Knowing that 83 percent of remote-working shoppers are going to talk about your brand with someone else is a huge advantage. It makes them a much more valuable acquisition as they contribute meaningfully to the acquisition of another customer.

Covid Has Changed Shoppers' Priorities

The last data points to discuss in this chapter are those that reflect how Covid's different impacts are affecting shoppers' attitudes. As we discussed in the chapter on corporate social responsibility, shoppers are becoming more heavily invested in how the companies behind the brands are behaving—both as good environmental stewards and fair, just employers. With all of this research going on, shoppers are learning more about brands than they ever knew before. They are learning about more than products, ingredients, and formulas. They are paying attention to a company's supply chain. Are these parts being sourced ethically? Is child or underpaid labor part of the manufacturing process? Did bribes have to be paid to corrupt officials to get this ingredient into my pantry?

Shoppers are also looking at a brand's environmental impact, both in terms of their safety practices but also their impact on global climate change. On top of both of those heavy topics, shoppers are now also reviewing companies' employment practices. Are they allowing workers to unionize? Have there been stories coming out about unsafe working conditions, unfair labor practices, or underpaid and overworked employees?

Our remote workers, who are doing the most research, are also coming across more of these stories. As a result, they claim to have higher expectations of conduct for the companies from which they buy. When asked how important each of the issues listed in Table 11.2 is to them, remote workers were significantly more likely than unemployed and on-site workers to say yes across every metric.

TABLE 11.2   Percentage of remote workers answering affirmatively that the issues are important to them

Protects users' personal data	**61%**
Passion for customer satisfaction	**60%**
Treating their employees well	**58%**
Supporting the local economy	**53%**
Making a positive difference in the world in which we live	**52%**
Environmentally responsible	**50%**
Transparent business practices	**50%**
Innovative and forward thinking	**49%**
Equality for gender, race, sexual orientation, etc.	**49%**
Providing affordable healthcare to their employees	**47%**
Giving back to charity	**46%**
Practices organic/non-GMO farming	**43%**

That is a very challenging list for a company to live up to! Beyond the behaviors and practices of an organization, remote workers are also significantly more likely to have stronger attitudes about how they "vote" with their wallets (Table 11.3).

Remote workers have crafted a shopper "identity" that prioritizes companies, brands, and products that allow them to feel like they are making an environmentally friendly and socially fair choice. Now, being realistic for a moment, we understand that this is self-reported data and people are going to put their best foot forward on surveys when it comes to claims about their behavior and morals. What matters to us is not the overall size of the

TABLE 11.3   Percentage of remote workers agreeing with the statement

I always buy products that are all natural or organic	**60%**
I care about the impact a product has on the environment	**57%**
I'm willing to pay more to make my shopping experience more convenient	**55%**
I need to know as much as I can about the manufacturing practices of the brands I buy	**41%**

number, but how remote workers are *significantly more likely* to say so than their on-site and unemployed peers. Assuming that it is in every human's nature to inflate their sense of self when asked questions like this, the gap in the data suggests that remote workers have the luxury of giving more weight to these issues.

The story that our data tells perfectly dovetails with the broader trends seen in a K-shaped recovery. Those that are well positioned to take advantage of the time, in this case our remote workers, will benefit from the current economic situation. They get to take their time, hunt out deals, experiment with new brands and products, and enjoy the shopping experience more. Covid has not been some great equalizer that unified shoppers into one hive mind. Rather, it further fractured us into different groups with vastly different shopping mindsets.

KEY TAKEAWAYS

- The Covid-19 pandemic is not equalizing our society. Instead, it highlights and even exacerbates existing inequalities. Those inequalities, both economic and psychological, are reflected in consumer behavior.

- Remote workers have an advantage over those whose jobs were lost or unaffected by Covid because they gained the luxury of more time and enjoyed uninterrupted income. As a result, they are more demanding and discerning shoppers.

- Those who work remotely have also become a valuable, high-income target market that is more likely to refract, or promote, a good brand experience. However, they are also more likely to defect to a competitor.

- Brands need to understand the makeup of their shopper population and address those shoppers' needs accordingly.

References

Alter Agents (2021) *Facing Fear: Overcoming consumer anxiety.*
    https://alteragents.com/wp-content/uploads/2021/01/Facing-Fear-III-full-res.pdf
    (archived at https://perma.cc/ZSP3-G9F7)
Capital One Insights Center (2021) *The Road to Recovery: 2021 Report.*
    https://ecm.capitalone.com/WCM/stories/pdfs/capital_one_insights_center_the_
    road_to_recovery_2021_report.pdf (archived at https://perma.cc/JEJ2-XRTW)

12

Strategies for Change

So you've been with us for eleven chapters. We're glad to have you on this journey through space and time. Thanks for being with us. This book is built off a decade of our experience around shopper decision making and how shoppers go from undecided to decided. We began this book by talking about how our story began—with a new methodology for marketers to understand how decision making was changing in a digitally empowered world. We shared our process of developing a new kind of research tool, one that broke many rules of research orthodoxy but opened up a new understanding of what it means to influence shopper decisions.

In the years since, we have studied the decision journey for numerous categories—vitamins, pet food, coffee, quickserve restaurants, financial services, travel, headphones, diabetes treatment, baby food, automotive, makeup, apparel, mobile phones, and many others. We shared the heat maps that helped us illustrate the ways in which the path to purchase was changing and pinpointing where influence actually takes place. We have shared hundreds of data points to demonstrate how there is no longer a linear journey from undecided to decided. We have revealed just how savvy shoppers have become, how expert they are at using wide swaths of information to make them smarter and more confident than ever before. We have described the ways in which we map the moment the shopper begins to consider making a purchase until the moment they hand over their money. We have shared our methodology around Source Usage, Net Influence, Source Content, Timeline, and Barriers. We have discussed the ways in which each of these differ by cohorts such as category, generation, gender, income, remote work, and those who have been impacted by Covid-19.

Hopefully through all of this, our key message—that shoppers want and need more content than ever before—has stuck. Because it's no longer enough for brands to promote a logo or an identity. Now, they must be content creators and news writers engaging with influencers and empowering shoppers to evangelize on their behalf. They must powerfully activate across dozens of touchpoints. They must inform shoppers with every detail they need to feel good about their decisions to buy their brand's products and services. And returning to two of the key findings from our Google ZMOT research: there is no linear path to purchase and every category can be a high consideration category.

As we have demonstrated, a critical consequence of shoppers being more informed than ever before is that they are more promiscuous than ever before. When they start their decision journey, they're much more open to new brands, new experiences, new everything. And this has caused them to re-evaluate all their decisions, even ones we might have called routine. Take the milk category. A decade ago Devora had a conversation with a skeptical milk board executive. The milk executive told her, "No one thinks about milk before they buy it. It's a habitual purchase. How can your methodology possibly apply to rote purchases?" Devora talked her ear off for an hour that day, but she wasn't able to convince her that it could. But 10 years later, think about your milk aisle. In addition to whole and lowfat milk there are now at least a dozen other milk alternatives for shoppers to consider: oat, almond, cashew, coconut, rice milk, macadamia, pea protein, lactose free, hemp milk, goat's milk, and there's even camel milk for newborns (really). Shoppers have been trained to accept the rapid pace of innovation since the last time they bought in a particular category, so they enter the category expecting innovations in flavors, ingredients, features, products, or even sustainable packaging. All of this illustrates that we're in a new world when it comes to marketing and researching shopper behavior.

Key truths we have revealed include:

- Shoppers are not passively waiting on you to inform them about your brand.
- Shoppers are hungry for and actively "hunt" for information.
- Shoppers perceive much less risk in trying new brands and products than they used to.
- Because of the volume of information available to them, shoppers are far more thoughtful than they used to be. While they may be willing to try new brands and products, they do more research than ever before. This is especially true of Millennial and Gen Z shoppers and remote workers.

- Shoppers expect transparency and thorough information to help them come to a decision with confidence.

- Shoppers expect innovation. A brand will fail if they are not rapidly updating and innovating in their space.

- The world was changing rapidly before the Covid-19 pandemic, but we're now seeing not only an acceleration of online tools but also shifts in priorities, attitudes, and beliefs. These are not momentary adjustments. Shoppers are setting out on a new behavioral path that's still evolving. If brands truly want to win with the promiscuous shopper, they have to orient their entire organization around a new understanding of shopper behavior.

We must acknowledge there is no limit on the options available to shoppers and the impact this increased access to choice, innovation, and information has had on brands, retailers, and shopper brains. This transformation has resulted in a very different kind of shopper—an entirely new generation of shoppers, actually—while brand marketing and market research is based on an outmoded purchase model. This brings us to the shock of Shopper Promiscuity that brands are coming to terms with. And it's long past time for those of us in the market research industry to acknowledge our role in pushing our work beyond the "norm" that results in Brand Narcissism.

Let's admit the level of navel gazing we have allowed to become standard in our research questions, as if you're dealing with an insecure, self-involved date that we described earlier: *How did you hear about me? What do you like about me? How do I stack up against your other dates? Are you going to go on another date with me?*

So many of the questions that we ask around the purchase funnel are from the brands' perspective but really don't reflect the shopper's experience. Because our research finds that almost half of all shoppers no longer go into a decision-making process with a brand in mind. They are coming in with their own needs, priorities, and how they want to solve the problem that they have. The two forces of Brand Narcissism and Shopper Promiscuity are inextricable and have created a perfect storm.

And here's our Jerry Maguire moment, our cry for a change in research. We are asking the wrong questions of a population that has fundamentally changed. The ship we've built out of traditional research cannot withstand the power of the coming storm brought on by Shopper Promiscuity. We are sounding the alarm on Shopper Promiscuity and revealing that traditional research is not helping us. The emperor has no clothes.

What To Do About It

So how do marketers meet shoppers where they are? How do you as a brand marketer, researcher, marketing executive, or CEO adjust to this new landscape? We have a few ideas. We'll start with what everyone ought to do, then break it down into next steps for researchers and marketers, and then offer a few suggestions for executives and CEOs.

Whoever you are, at whatever stage of development your brand is, whatever role you play in your particular company, here are five strategies to consider and some examples of brands we think are doing it well:

1 **Feed information-hungry shoppers.** Put information everywhere—on packaging, websites, third party retail sites, social media, and online videos. Provide transparency, details, and reviews. People are looking for information and a decent percentage will exhaust every avenue to learn more. Not every source of information can be comprehensive, but always make your information accessible, credible, and clear. Lego is a perfect example of a brand that went all-in on YouTube and online videos. Not every brand will be able to reach over four million subscribers and 5.5 billion views, but they set the bar for what can be achieved by sharing information through interviews with brand designers and product managers. The brand's October 2021 video on the Lego Queer Eye's Fab Five Loft set is a prime example of the level of depth that shoppers are increasingly seeking from brands.

2 **Do not assume loyalty or even repeat trial.** Today's shopper can be perfectly happy with a product and still be interested in exploring new brands the next time they're in the market. Loyalty does not carry the power it once had. You only have to look at the success of disruptors like Dollar Shave Club or Blue Apron to realize that shoppers are eager to explore. If your brand relies on shelf space and nostalgia to hit their sales goals, you're going to be caught in that perfect storm and find it hard to stay afloat.

3 **Be wary of "loyalty metrics" in your data.** Whether you're looking at repeat purchases, ticket size, or Net Promoter, always know that these only tell part of the story. Most loyalty metrics look at a point in time and do not follow shoppers for the long term. That shopper who claimed loyalty in your last survey might be the first to defect to another brand the next time they shop. For true brand health, you also need to look at the cost of customer acquisition, shopper attitudes in your category, and,

most importantly, Shopper Promiscuity metrics. Kodak had strong loyalty scores, high brand awareness, and strong brand personality metrics until the iPhone moved digital photography into a whole new realm.

4 **Stay focused on the future.** We've trained shoppers to expect rapid growth—especially in the last 10 to 15 years as smartphone technology launched a whole new era of accessibility. *The Innovator's Dilemma* (Christensen, 2011) has never been more relevant than it is right now. Anticipate shopper needs and address them before the shopper knows they need it. What makes this even more essential is that competition might come from a blind spot. Just like Kodak was surprised by the iPhone, so has Marriott been deeply challenged by Airbnb. It is no longer about staying at the forefront of your category, but seeing where challenges are coming from far afield. Lululemon is a great example of a sportswear company that has both created and expanded the category it serves. With its 2020 purchase of the virtual exercise platform Mirror, Lululemon demonstrated yet again its ability to pivot and expand through innovation.

5 **Be hyper-adaptive.** Use the lessons from the Covid-19 pandemic to ask: What if we had to change everything overnight? New black swan events are always on the horizon, including the growing climate emergency, potential future pandemics, supply chain issues, and economic crashes. Have strategies in place to keep your brand thriving during turbulent times. Keep your organization nimble and proactive. We've seen many larger brands address change through re-orgs and meetings to build strategies, but this is often started late and designed to take time. Meanwhile, their competitors are moving the goal posts even further away. Exercise class app Mindbody took this on at the start of the Covid-19 pandemic by allowing users to expand from classes in their area and take a virtual class from anywhere in the world. Gaming platform Twitch adapted during the pandemic by expanding from gaming and esports to being a place for live DJ sets and concerts. National and local grocery stores moved to curbside pickups and same day delivery when it was clear the pandemic was going to go longer than a two-week lockdown. That same kind of "pandemic energy" needs to be the norm in the future.

Ok, so that's the high-level wrap up. But now, let's look at what it means for distinct leaders in any organization. We'll start with the research team, since that's our home territory.

Next Steps for Researchers

If you're a researcher, maybe you head up consumer insights, maybe you represent the voice of the shopper, or perhaps you work in the customer experience—whatever area of focus you have, first of all, we salute you with a deep bow. Thank you for all you do—thank you for working late to find the most critical truths that really matter, thank you for speaking truth to power and telling your organization "*I know you think that is a good idea, but the consumers aren't feeling it.*" Or "*This social media algorithm, it's hurting more than helping.*" Thank you for identifying that sustainability matters—and then digging in to find out how and why. Thank you for being the ones to reveal how to best serve shoppers and how to be better partners to your customers. We see you, we acknowledge you, and we know how hard it is to do this job well.

Of all the folks who read this book, you're probably the most likely to be responsible for carrying out these findings. And you might feel a little overwhelmed at this moment. We've tackled a lot of topics, including things that touch on core parts of your work and which are, in some cases, highly political—such as the brand tracker that is both sacred and, at times, despised. We've suggested we rethink that methodology completely and replace it with a new approach that requires a whole new set of questions. However, hopefully, we have also given you some ideas that enliven and re-invigorate your research methods. So let's start there, with a list of suggested actions for both research and marketing teams.

1 **Mix modal research forever.** We live in a dynamic world that only becomes more fragmented and complex every year. Given this, traditional, single method research is often not enough to answer emerging questions like "*What's the future of the retail store?*" or "*What's the impact of augmented reality on shopping?*" or "*What values matter to shoppers after two years of a global pandemic?*" To address the complex questions, consider applying multi-modal studies that involve both quantitative stated data and neuroscience or qualitative interviews. New technologies allow us to do this more efficiently and cost-effectively than ever before.

2 **Explore neuroscience.** Neuroscience is closer than ever to being at parity with more traditional qualitative and quantitative methodologies in terms of reliability and scalability. This is still a young science and a new method to add to your research toolkit, but start now before your

competitors begin leading with insights you won't uncover for another ten years. Even if you just dip your toe in, begin playing with neuro marketing solutions to expand your comfort with answering tough questions in new ways.

3 **Shake up your brand tracker.** We get that your marketing and executive teams may rely on your brand equity and ad trackers in a way that makes it impossible to do away with them completely. That is a reality that many of our clients face as well. But there are steps that can be taken to bring richer and more accurate insights into your organization, with the hope that one day they'll be seen for the value they provide and put the brand tracker out to pasture. One step is to do a "narcissism audit" by looking at how your questions are asked, who they are asked of, and what you are truly learning from the data.

4 **Bring big data and market research together.** There were a couple of years in the mid-2000s when all you heard at any conference was "*Big data, big data, big data.*" Even we had a moment where we wondered, will research be replaced by the data companies have in their own systems? That's not what happened, because as Cheryl Idell, VP of Global Consumer Insights at Netflix reminds us, now more than ever, "there is a need for consumer insights to partner with and make sense of big data. Data science teams and consumer insights teams have got to become much more connected because the data science doesn't tell you the *why*. It doesn't even tell you a lot about the *who*. But particularly the *why*, that's the piece you will see results spit out in a data table that you can't interpret, unless you actually talk to consumers to understand what's behind the behavior, what caused the behavior." Cheryl anticipates a new name for this approach will emerge: "At Netflix, we've combined our teams so that consumer insights and data science are folded into an org called 'data and insights' because of the importance of always having the yin and yang of those two."

5 **Validate and revalidate your understanding of your consumer target.** If you're doing general population or targeted studies of your presumed audience, chances are you are missing the opportunity to identify new communities that may be interested in your offering. Online research often skews heavily female, white, and higher income. And yet Hispanic and African American audiences are critical cohorts who may be poorly served by your marketing—in part because they are not sufficiently represented in your research. Additionally, our customers are self-identifying

in new ways that create dynamic and fascinating cohorts to study. Go talk to them, augment your quant sample, and get to know other communities who may be either underserved or under connected. As USC Professor and experienced brand marketer Gil Guttierez, says, "To win and continue to 'seduce' vs your competition will require a nuanced knowledge of your consumer unlike what has been necessary in the past. In other words, a lot of research. In a world of fragmented media and multiple channels, reaching out to this consumer will require a lot of advertising and production. Namely, there's a lot of cost here, you want to make sure you're investing in the right consumers."

6 **Look at what's not working for shoppers.** If your team conducts customer satisfaction studies, be sure you are evaluating whether these satisfaction metrics are inherently narcissistic. Are you looking at an exhaustive list of barriers—and asking shoppers which ones are the hardest barriers for them to get over? Are you actually revealing what is working for shoppers or are you looking at what your team decided was worthwhile asking about? Are you willing to take on what's actually causing barriers for shoppers, or just what you are willing to fix? If you're not taking this on with complete and total commitment, count on the fact that your competitors will.

7 **Keep an eye on evolving shopper values and what it means for your brand.** Shoppers are keenly aware of the inequities and injustices in our system. Their expectations have shifted dramatically in the past few years, and as challenges such as climate emergencies and social justice take on a greater urgency, they will demand brands put a stake in the ground. Consider building values, sustainability, and disruption into your ongoing research initiatives so they are not one-off studies but truly integrated into your understanding of consumer and shopper needs.

8 **Communicate your findings more effectively and create a seat for yourself at the table.** One key challenge many researchers face is how to effectively engage stakeholders and make them champions of research programs. Much has been said about the importance of data and insights storytelling but it's worth repeating here: you can't effectively serve the shopper if the marketing or executive teams are not listening to the shopper through your research findings. Learn how to communicate research insights effectively and fight for a seat at the table with executive teams so that the voice of the shopper is not the last place brands come to but the first.

9 **Rethink research in the post-pandemic age.** The Covid-19 pandemic forced many industries to rethink their business models, practices, and protocol from the ground up. The market research industry is no exception. While more and more research was being done online, focus groups and qualitative research were still primarily conducted in person. However, with in-person research shut down for almost two years, it's forced researchers to get creative. Again, Cheryl Idell from Netflix: "The pandemic in many ways was a bit of a blessing for research and has made us better. It doesn't mean we don't ever want to be in a room with people. Being brought into people's homes virtually can reveal things that we may not have even seen in person. That's been a blessing because I think a lot of researchers would have really taken a much slower path to getting to this. And I don't see a world where we go back to anywhere near the volume of in-person qualitative work that we used to do." Most researchers share this view—there will have to be a good reason to go back to in-person methods. It saves time and money and may allow research teams to stretch their budgets while expanding their sample size. Consider what scenarios still justify in-person research and explore exciting new qualitative alternatives emerging like Dscout, Remesh, or Recollective.

Next Steps for Marketers

1 **Evaluate the category you're actually playing in.** With more vying for the attention of consumers and shoppers than ever before, sometimes you're not only competing against your presumed competitive set but may be up against forces outside of your category. For example, if you work for a professional sports team trying to sell tickets and advertising for live games, you may assume you're competing with other teams and sports franchises. But in today's economy, you're also competing with entertainment, social media, and a wide range of content that consumers have to choose from in their own homes. It's not enough to be the best in your lane—you've got to provide value that extends to other areas your target audience may be spending their time in.

2 **Examine unexplored channels and touchpoints.** Use the approach we have shared to identify marketing channels you may not be leveraging correctly. Whether it's an organic video strategy or podcaster influencer

or direct mail campaign, uncover what the sources of influence are that may not even be on your marketing roadmap and see if it makes a difference.

3 **Use Source Usage and Net Influence to unpack your competitor marketing plans.** Beyond identifying where to invest your brand dollars, use Source Usage and Net Influence to identify where your competitors are putting their investments. Instead of focusing on comparing your brand awareness vs theirs, see what sources shoppers are actually using and whether you can learn anything from shopper insights to help you be more strategic in your investments. Maybe you'll uncover that your competitors have an unexpected promotion strategy, or are being more effective with their point of sale investments. Whatever they are doing, you can gain insight into their marketing investments through the power of Source Usage and Net Influence.

4 **Use the Shopper DIAL to uncover your category's Shopper Promiscuity rating, and find new segments of shoppers to pursue.** Every category differs in terms of Shopper Promiscuity, research engagement, promotional activity, and other factors that influence shopper decisions. Knowing the landscape of your category can make an enormous difference. Get a handle on the level of Shopper Promiscuity in your category and then build strategies around that information. This will allow you to identify which shoppers may be up for grabs or willing to convert. Finally, thinking about those promiscuous explorer shoppers, marketer Gil Guttierez says, "Keep track of the 'oenologists' of your category as a way of tracking where preference is heading. They're the 'canary in the coal mine.' These 'oenologists' are likely the best advocates of your brand if you can seduce them."

5 **Incorporate influence into your media metrics.** Look at the metrics that your marketing dashboard offers and identify whether there is a missing metric that tells you not only the number of people doing something but the level of influence these sources have on purchase. Then consider adding "influence" on purchase as a key tool in your media metrics toolbox.

6 **Evaluate content from the shopper's point of view and expand your content marketing efforts.** Ask your research team to study shoppers and how they make decisions in your category. Then evaluate your marketing and ad content to see if it's actually answering shoppers' questions. Learn to put the right content in front of the shoppers where *they* are going to

look for that information. Make shopper education a strategic investment. Apply content marketing as a powerful means to achieve that goal.

7 **Make sure your brand is not a narcissist.** Conduct an audit into your
marketing campaigns. Are you behaving like a brand narcissist? Are you
talking mostly about you and the stuff you want to talk about? Or do
your campaigns reflect that you have listened to your shoppers and are
able to actually meet shoppers where they are?

8 **Unpack Shopper Promiscuity.** There's no way to operate effectively
without accepting the reality that shoppers are more promiscuous than
ever before and this will only continue to grow for future generations.
Coming to terms with this new paradigm quickly will position your
brand to succeed in the future. Starting now, your brand can orient
towards Shopper Promiscuity, understand what motivates shoppers to
change brands, look at opportunities you have to pull shoppers away
from competitors, and future proof against unseen threats.

Next Steps for Executives and CEOs

When initially planning out this chapter, we had planned to have a third
section of next steps for executives and CEOs with a lengthy list of actionable bullets. But everything we wrote down was simply a variation of support. Support your research and marketing teams in every possible way.
They are facing new challenges and have to be more adaptive, innovative,
and creative than ever before. What does full support look like?

1 **Provide proper funding.** Your teams need to be spending money wisely,
but to do that they need the knowledge on where and how their marketing dollars are most effective. That means funding research to get those
answers. We could write a whole other book about the importance of
funding research, but the bottom line is, to be successful in a complex and
competitive market, you need to understand and talk regularly to the
people buying your stuff—and the people who might but who you haven't
even identified. There are also implications for hiring on your marketing
team. If the marketing team doesn't have the resources or right functions
to activate on research findings, it won't be possible to blunt the competition.

2 **Be an internal cheerleader.** Give consumer insights a seat at the table.
Without them there, your executive team is making decisions in the dark.

Shoppers are rapidly evolving and if you don't know what is happening with them now, you'll plan the wrong products and marketing for the future. Create a Chief Insights Officer role immediately, and watch how much more informed your leadership team can be with regular access to the person whose job it is to be the voice of the customer in all meetings.

3 **Use the insights.** This seems obvious. Why invest in research and insights, bring them into the room and then ignore the findings? We've seen it happen more than we'd like. The reason is because the answers can be uncomfortable, inconvenient, and force disruption. That is all the more reason to lean into them and do the work.

4 **Surviving and thriving in a world of Shopper Promiscuity is absolutely possible.** But to do so, we need the narcissism industrial complex to be dismantled. Research teams must move beyond loyalty and purchase funnels and start learning how things are done from the shopper's point of view. Marketers need to get comfortable with promiscuous shopping and find ways to elevate their brands in this new ecosystem. CEOs need to build growth strategies based on shopper needs and priorities, not narcissistic metrics. Influencing shopper decisions in this new age requires new thinking and approaches that always put the shopper at the center of everything.

Reference

Christensen, C (2011) *The Innovator's Dilemma: The revolutionary book that will change the way you do business*, HarperBusiness, New York

INDEX

Page numbers in *italic* indicate Figures and those in **bold** indicate Tables.